The Working Woman's Dream House

The Working Woman's Dream House

A Design, Building, and Remodeling Guide

John S. M. Hamilton, Architect

BETTERWAY PUBLICATIONS, INC.
WHITE HALL, VIRGINIA

Published by Betterway Publications, Inc.
P.O. Box 219
Crozet, VA 22932
(804) 823-5661

Cover design and photograph by Susan Riley
Photographs by the author, Mark Boisclair, Dave Davis, and Susan Riley
Text illustrations by James R. Schnirel
Typography by East Coast Typography, Inc.

Library of Congress Cataloging-in-Publication

Hamilton, John S. M.
       The working woman's dream house : a design and remodeling guide/
John S. M. Hamilton/
             p.   cm.
       Includes index.
       ISBN 1-55870-132-X.
       1. Dwellings–Remodeling.   2. Women—Time management.
I. Title / TH4816.H2883   1989
643'.7—dc2o

                                                        89-36133
                                                           CIP

Printed in the United States of America
0 9 8 7 6 5 4 3 2

For Blanche, Helen, Sue, Jenny, and Lisa

Acknowledgments

This book is about creating a home that will offer efficiency, beauty, and the pleasures you deserve. The intent was to provide a publication of lasting value. Many people contributed to that effort.

Norman Mayer furnished valuable editing with helpful and kind commentary. Jim Schnirel produced the fine sketches needed to supplement my text.

Sue Hamilton's ever-present encouragement and thoughtful critiques were constructive and always timely. This "working woman" always finds time to be there when needed.

Trisha Morgan typed the manuscript, again magically transforming my writing to a legible state.

I am grateful to the following women for their comments and ideas. Their contribution is reflected in every chapter of this book:

Linda Ackerman, Donna M. Alexander, Pat Anderberg, Marcia Ashley, Debra J. Augustyn, Dolores Augustyn, Janet Augustyn, Wendy Augustyn, Judith Baer, Judy Baker, Lisa Baker, Rose Batina, Marjorie F. Becking, Shirley A. Bender, Grace Block, Leslee Bowen, Mrs. J. Bromfield, Claire Bumpers, Jenny Carter, Joan Caruso, Trudy L. Charlton, Patricia Chreech, B. A. Christensen, Patricia Coffin, Char Cole, Sue Collins, Janet Currah, Geri Dahle, Donna Davies, Terri R. Davies, Dorthina Davis, Mona Demaline, Diane Devine, Arline Diskin, Carolyn Doran, Judi Duenes, Vern Duff, Frances Elliott, Carole Fatzinger, Rosemary Fetterolf, Dianne Foster, Patricia J. Froelich, Nancy Fulmer, Lisa Green, Sally Ann Greenwood, Helen Goldsmith, Elaine Gruver, Lisa Hamilton, Lynne Hamilton, Maria Hauser, Marti Hays, Mary Lou Hentges, Shirley A. Hill, C. Hillow, Patricia Himel, Sandra L. Hodgeman, Heidi K. Horwitz, Anne Howarth, Joyce Howarth, Carol Hurt, Carol Jenkins, Mary P. Johnson, Sandy Johnson, Helen Jones, Janet Kane, Audrie Kemp, Janet Kenney, Judi Ketchum, Myrna King, Linda Klinger, Erica Langley, Peggy Lay, Betty Lightner, Margaret Loose, Beth Lounsbury, Mary Lynch, Marilyn P. McDonald, Catherine McGann, Norma McLain, Dorothy Marino, Karen Moore, Kim Moore, Trisha A. Morgan, Adalee Muse, S. Diane Nofs, Beth Norris, Sharon Odom, J. Petersen, Kathy Pizzello, Nancy Russell Plencner, Jane Pullaro, Elea Raiswell, Elizabeth A. Rasband, Judy Robertson, Donna Rogers, Patty Russell, J. Rutledge, Diane Ryan, Georgia Salwitz, Dee Sams, Ethel P. Sanden, Vicki Savage, Cristal Sawyer, Cozee Schabaker, Shirley Schnirel, Helen Seville, Patricia Skelpsa, Amy Smith, Donna K. Smith, Jan Snyder, Nancy C. Stanula, Anne Steele, Pamela H. Steffes, Carrie Stone, Sherie Street, Glenna Teel, Chris Thiltgen, M. Thomas, Irene Timmy, Linda Turk, Margaret Walker, Barbara Watson, Ellen Watson, Gay Whetman, Carolyn Williams, Elaine Wozneak, and Marge Zabukovic.

Contents

Introduction
It Can Be Yours

The "Working Woman's Dream House" can be YOUR HOME . . . future or existing. This book tells you how to make it happen.

It's all within your reach. Whether building, buying, or remodeling, the *potential for having your own dream house is far greater than you ever imagined.*

If you are remodeling, the right alterations can create the beauty, convenience, features, and pleasure you deserve. If you're building a new house, read on, and *believe* you can have the home you've always wanted.

If you are buying a house, the same ideas apply when you know what to look for.

Having a home that you can't wait to get back to — one that gives you pleasure and contentment — is not wishing for the moon. It's not just for the other person. It's very achievable, and *you can have it!*

My objective is to make your home more beautiful, efficient, and a sheer joy to live in. You will spend less time on "required" tasks. Together, we will increase convenience, pleasure, and quality time at home.

The focus will be on remodeling as well as new construction. It's meant for *every* woman — whether she works outside the home full-time or part-time, or is a full-time homemaker. But there is a catch — it won't happen by accident. *You have to get involved in the process!* This book will tell you how.

GET INVOLVED

I have received many comments from women who knew I was writing this book. The following quotation is worth noting: "Good luck. It's very nice to see a male architect want to consider a woman's feelings about design. I have seen very little in home design that has a woman's viewpoint reflected."

Well, as in all things, that is a two-sided affair. It's time for you, the woman, to share the responsibility — to get involved!

I have been designing new homes and remodeling old ones for twenty-five years. My pre-design discussions with homeowners are always extensive and I ask for input from all parties living in the home. Too often, however, the woman does not make specific requests for much beyond the basic areas — a few appliances, fixtures, certain colors, and maybe something about the master bedroom and bath.

When building new or remodeling, you must state your point of view and make your objectives, needs, and wishes known to whomever is directing the design. Don't generalize when you should be specific. Discuss your lifestyle. Include your thoughts on home management, cleanability, and efficiency. If you are an experienced homemaker, draw on your experience. If it's your first home, talk to other women, and get their advice. *You must then furnish the information needed by the designer to create your special environment.*

ACHIEVE A BALANCE

Home is your most important environment. With that in mind, seek to create a home that brings pleasure to your senses — a home that will be a refuge and sanctuary. Those objectives share equal value with the more practical aspects of home design. Creating that important balance will be discussed throughout the book.

THE QUESTIONNAIRE

Even with twenty-five years of successful home design, I didn't have all the answers. Before beginning this book, I surveyed women across the country, sending each one a questionnaire intended to cover most areas and functions of their homes.

Replies came from Florida to Washington, Maine to California, and some from Canada. A bonus to me were many comments supporting thoughts already planned for the book — plus some replies that set me thinking in new areas.

Throughout the book, I use the survey comments liberally. These comments are identified as quotations.

In addition to the survey results and my experience as an architect, I have had a close relationship with a working woman for twenty-six years — my wife. We built our present home fifteen years ago. She is nice enough to say it's "almost perfect."

HABIT

In a previous book, *Discover Your Dream House*, I talked about the "habit trap." Too many of us accept the design of our home as irrevocable, assuming that changes are too expensive or too much trouble. Time and again, responses I get reinforce this. We are all guilty of doing things by rote. We don't consider how to improve the quality of our lives.

You *can* improve that quality of life. You *can* increase efficiency. You *can* make pleasure the

mainstay in your home environment. Often it's easy and takes only a minor change, but it doesn't just happen; *you* must do it.

A SURVEY PLUS

One of the best (and rarest) survey comments came from a woman living in Utah, with a husband and three young children. "I love my home! It's a great space to live and work in." That quotation was written in answer to the question: "What are the irritating areas of your home?"

Her other comments included the following: "Open kitchen with lots of light — a pleasure to be in. Bathroom with skylight. Master bedroom — large, open to outside with sitting room feeling. Kitchen/family room — all open to outside, decks and yard. Lots of light — windows."

There is a common denominator within these comments. They all relate to the *atmosphere* of her home! She did not mention areas difficult to clean, poor traffic patterns, terrible storage, etc. She may have those problems and more. But, in response to my questions, the elements of her home that created good feelings overpowered any practical deficiencies that existed.

I don't make light of the need for easy cleaning, maintenance, and manageability. After all, that is one reason for this book. I simply mean to stress the *need for a balance*. To increase quality time at home requires a balance of *all* the elements of good design. *Your home should be so easy to maintain that leisure time is abundant. However, when you do have time to enjoy the atmosphere of your home, let's make sure there is some!*

The home that is best for you may not resemble the one described above. That doesn't matter, and doesn't relate to our objective here. *Your* home should be customized to *your* priorities. So my objective is to help you reach the point where you can say, "I love my home! It's a great space to live and work in."

1
Dream House Created

The title "Dream House" is not one I'm naturally comfortable with. It has about it the illusion of a wonderful place that is found, rather than created — the hint of the fairy tale. That's not the way it works.

Chances are you, as a house shopper, won't find that one in a million "just right" place without making alterations. You will create your "Dream House" — either through alteration or building from scratch.

THE DESIGN PROCESS

Good design does *not* require being "different," using trendy materials, or making architectural "statements." Good home design creates aesthetic pleasure; it will enhance your lifestyle and satisfy functional needs.

This requires planning. Planning means to define those needs and establish your priorities first, before actual design even begins.

The opposite approach is aptly defined by a woman in New York: "Every time we build or remodel we think of something we should have done, or wish we had done, when it's too late!"

Custom Planning

Most subdivision housing is created for the "mass market." It's seldom customized for a specific homeowner. If you live in this type of home and want to improve it — YOU CAN. The trick is to identify the problem *before* trying to solve it.

The best approach is to determine the *highest priorities* among all your needs and wishes. It's not complicated, and with this book it will be even easier.

To improve your home, first get to know how you live within it. You may be surprised at what you learn. You need to recognize which areas or features give you benefit or pleasure and which are irritating. Start writing them down. Keep a check list. Define your likes, dislikes, living habits, and needs.

What situations and features cause you to spend time in cleaning and maintenance — time that could be spent more enjoyably? What labor-saving conveniences do you have? What conveniences do you wish you had?

These questions — and more — should be addressed. When you do, it's amazing how quickly solutions for improvement present themselves. NOTE: I have provided a short check list at the end of this chapter for your reference.

THE HABIT TRAP

In response to my Questionnaire, this comment came from a woman in Toronto: "Having given this some thought, I have decided that I am an adapter." She is not alone.

Think about the patterns in your daily routine that have become habit. Habit isn't always based on desire, but often on the fact that you have been force-fit into the house. With a house not designed for you, *you adapt to it.*

It's not hard to spot habit traps resulting from bad design, and here are some examples: (1) the traffic pattern interrupts room functions (a Virginia woman said, "All traffic coming in the front door must pass through the living room to reach other areas"); (2) kitchen work takes too long because of a poor layout and bad storage; (3) your laundry area is in the wrong part of the house; (4) poor planning has robbed you of a place for privacy — to unwind and collect your thoughts; (5) you are missing a nice view that could have been there with a different design. Possible examples are endless.

Involuntary habit clouds your thinking about potential for home improvement. Becoming aware of those "force-fit" habits helps you to break out of the rut and creates an objective, fresh approach. As you read through these chapters, think about reducing the work and irritation based on habit.

Focus on things that make your home an exciting and fun place to be. Features like flowing space, good light, the inside and outside relationship, are some simple examples. Another is a house plan that allows and encourages interaction with family members. An example of that is a kitchen/family space that lets you be part of the action while preparing dinner.

THE BIG PICTURE

Without question, a basic purpose in home planning is to create convenience and ease cleaning needs. Your time is too valuable to do otherwise. But keep the whole picture in sight. The total picture includes the need for your home to be a place of comfort, peace, and protection.

The pleasures of contentment, beauty, and a sense of repose come with planning that goes beyond utility. That planning should produce interesting design and delightful spaces. *With good design, you can have it all* — function, efficiency, utility, *and* aesthetic pleasure.

To that end, this chapter presents an overview looking at some features and ideas that make up the "big picture."

Quiet Places

If a design encouraging interaction is important to you, it's even better when balanced with optional private spaces. When asked what feature in her home was of most benefit, a Utah woman answered: "We have our separate areas to escape to."

Valuable is that niche, that quiet space for private detachment from the clamor and chaos of the world (or a noisy family). To have a place where you can take a step back — to recharge your batteries in quiet perspective — that is the pause that refreshes a busy life.

Private space activities are visual, audio, and psychological. Those needs can be met in private rooms or as part of a large multi-purpose space.

The need for "Quiet Space" in your home is so important that I have devoted a separate chapter to the subject.

Open and Closed Planning

Homes designed with "open planning" are in tune with much of today's living. Advantages to open planning are discussed in later chapters on Cleaning, Convenience, and Interaction.

An open plan will reduce the number of corners and walls to clean. It promotes interaction between people. It can create an airy, spacious feeling and make a small house appear roomier; however, it's not for everyone.

Comments received from a California woman explain why she prefers closed planning: "I much prefer a closed plan. It offers privacy. It also closes off rooms not totally cleaned up, i.e., the kitchen."

While the prevailing preference of women across the country is for open planning in certain areas — family interaction while working in the kitchen — it's basically a personal matter and deserves some thought before building or remodeling. A compromise using both open and closed planning is the typical result.

Color

The right color combinations do wonders for the "good feeling" that comes from being in certain homes.

The effect of color on atmosphere is an established fact. Color can make a space cheerful or dreary, warm or cold, even larger or smaller. It affects our subconscious state of mind.

If there could be only one guideline — to start off on the right foot — it would be off-white walls. The color is fresh, reflects light, and visually opens up tight spaces.

Other colors are introduced into a space by: carpet, baseboard, furnishings, and wall hangings. The contrast between those objects and lighter background walls is important. Lightness contrast contributes to pattern and spatial perception. The greater the contrast, the more likely is the chance for good color combinations.

Of course, someone good with colors can do the opposite of what I described above and do it well. Great spaces are possible with any combination of colors, from tomato-red walls to black gloss ceilings. It's all a matter of knowing how to do it.

Many people need help in color selection, if only to affirm the appropriateness of choice. If you are unsure of selections, by all means, seek opinions from a consultant.

The chapters on Light and Furnishings discuss different aspects of color.

STORAGE

Lack of storage is the *number one complaint* everywhere in the country. Typical interior needs are: (1) general storage around the house; (2) kitchen storage; (3) bedroom-dressing area storage.

Lack of storage creates clutter, and clutter creates irritation and extra work. The Storage chapter has guidelines to help plan and improve *your* storage.

Whether renovating or building a new house, the same rules apply. Household storage has improved little over the past thirty years. It will improve only when *you* force the improvement — when you refuse to buy a home without good storage.

WIPE OUT IRRITATION

Most household irritation is unnecessary. Let's wipe it out. Not all homes have the same irritations. Moreover, what irritates you may not bother someone else. Here are a few survey comments:

"Poor kitchen layout"
"Small rooms"
"Poor lighting"
"Small closets"
"Not enough storage"
"Must go through dining room & kitchen to get to the family room"
"Formal living room where no one goes except at Christmas"
"Hard to clean windows"
"Poor placement of electrical outlets"
"Dark kitchen"
"Fireplace positioned in a way that makes sitting near it impossible"
"Wall space inadequate for arranging furniture"
"No exit from basement"
"Poor traffic pattern"

And so it goes . . . on and on . . .

In fact, *many* of these items can be easily corrected without great imagination or expense. Most of us are in our own particular rut. Often, it's only a matter of DOING SOMETHING ABOUT IT!

This book presents ideas to help you meet

head-on the items on the above list, and more. Our goal is to erase irritation — to make your home easy to clean, maintain, and *enjoy*.

KITCHEN REVIEW

The kitchen is the most "built-in" space in your home. To change the way it functions usually requires actual reconstruction. Therefore, kitchen renovation is fairly expensive. The above statements support the notion that you should take more time with initial kitchen planning, to get it right the first time. (The chapters on Storage, Cleaning, Convenience and Interaction discuss kitchen design.)

Renovation of kitchens becomes more economical when you *spend the money in the right place*. It's amazing how many times I have been asked to redesign a kitchen that has been altered before.

Don't resist spending the time to define and itemize needs and wishes. It's not difficult; it's time well spent, and you need do it *only once*. (See the list of "Planning Considerations" in Chapter 5.) The bottom line is that you end up with a kitchen that is nice to be in.

GOOD PLANNING IS UP TO YOU

The following comments are typical of many I have received: (1) "Most homes are not designed for a woman (i.e., poor lighting in kitchen, small kid's bedroom, poor laundry location, bad kitchen layout, and bad location with the house)." (2) "Unfortunately, women work, clean, and are in the house more than men, but men are the ones who design the houses."

I will say again, get involved and assume your share of the responsibility for those problems.

If you are planning a new house or major renovation, *let the designer know your needs, desires, and living habits*. Don't accept a design that doesn't have the elements of practicality asked for — such as storage, efficient kitchen, good laundry location, easily maintained materials, etc. . . .

To complain after the fact is futile. It's too late! Get involved in the planning process.

**Reference Check List for
Design Basics in Your Home**

1. Where do you need storage most?
    a. Kitchen
    b. Bedroom
    c. Dressing & Wardrobe Area
    d. Laundry
    e. Other
2. What function or space would you like to add?
    a. Office/Study
    b. Hobby or Work Room (to leave messy if necessary)
    c. Extra storage in Bedroom or Wardrobe area
    d. Laundry/Utility Room
    e. Convenient storage, generally, throughout the home
    f. Other
3. What areas or features of your home give you the most benefit or pleasure?
4. a. What specific time/labor-saving home design conveniences or features do you have that are most helpful?
    b. What specific convenience or feature do you wish you had?
5. Where do you spend the most time? (Exclude actual sleeping time)
    a. Family Room/Den
    b. Kitchen
    c. Living Room
    d. Bedroom
    e. Bathroom/Dressing Area
    f. Other
6. Do you often watch TV while eating?
7. What are the irritating areas of your home? (For example: small closets, small rooms, poor lighting, kitchen layout, traffic pattern)

8. What would make housecleaning easier? (For instance: type of flooring, window covering, storage, furnishings, etc.)

9. a. Do you have any design features that enhance your interaction with other household members?

b. Do you want more interaction, such as when working in the kitchen?

10. Is pet care time consuming or inconvenient?

11. Does yard maintenance take too much time?

12. Now add your own comments.

2
Interaction

When asked what home design features give the most pleasure, a surprising number of women refer to features that enhance interaction with other people. Here are several examples:

"Kitchen open to other areas . . . to let people feel they are a part of what's going on — outside the kitchen as well as those in the kitchen."

"Family room, kitchen — one large room."

"Kitchen/family room together allows you to cook, watch or listen to TV, talk and relax in two of the busiest rooms in the house."

"A center island/work station in kitchen — including bar/counter with seats for guests."

"My friends tend to hover around the kitchen and having one that will accommodate that is important."

"I love my open kitchen/breakfast room, open to the family room."

The same point is brought home, in reverse, by a Seattle woman. Asked for the most *irritating* feature of her home, she said, "A small kitchen that is isolated from other areas of the house."

With young children, another way to interact and communicate is visibility from the kitchen to an outside play area. From a Massachusetts woman: "When the children were small, I could hear or see them most of the time from the kitchen."

MAKE CONTACT

Most working mothers want contact with the family when they get home. It's also true that most of you head for the kitchen, on arrival, to get the meal started. So, if your home has separate rooms with a closed-off kitchen, it may be time to open up and *make contact.*

TOGETHERNESS

Family contact, of course, also happens beyond the kitchen. A Pennsylvania woman described to me her dream room for family togetherness: "A room that is large enough for everyone to be doing something different. Instead of separate areas scattered around, if all are working in one area, there is bound to be more interaction — even if doing different things."

The space she describes — multi-function, living/family space — works well for some families. Some of the ways to achieve it are:

1. Changes in floor level (i.e., sunken or raised areas) or ceiling heights or both.
2. Provide variations in the plan for niches, bays, and alcoves.
3. Deviate from a square or rectangular plan to reduce sound reverberation.
4. Good acoustical absorption, which might include heavy carpet, soft furniture, and acoustical wall materials.

5. Plan several furniture arrangements catering to different functions. Design lighting to accommodate the separate areas.

THE GAME ROOM

Another gathering place is a "game room." Typically, it's a converted basement or an add-on specifically for that purpose.

That space offers a different type of advantage for many women. It's less for her interaction than knowing where everyone else is located. In my experience, a woman seldom asks for a game room — usually it's the man or the children. I hasten to add I see nothing wrong in that, it's just putting it in perspective.

MOVING THE ACTION OUTSIDE

Family fun is any place you can make it happen. Outside spaces, planned with care, are a sure bet.

The screened-in porch, in certain climates, is a natural for the summer months. It's a perfect location for indoor-outdoor interaction. Other climates don't need screened spaces and covered patios do the job.

Outside deck areas provide aesthetic pleasure as well as people places. Here is a quote from a Connecticut woman: "The design of our backyard is comfortable and secluded. The deck area, away from the house, is shaded by trees and very private. It's a place to go in the spring, summer, and fall to chat with family members and relax."

NOT FOR EVERYONE

The open plan promotes people contact, but it's not for everyone. A woman in northern California expressed it this way: "Our dining room is open to the living room. Usually it's nice, but you must clear the area immediately after a meal because the mess is not conducive to 'gracious entertaining'."

If that fits your situation, consider opening the plan in another way. Have the kitchen open to a more casual family area, or expand the kitchen to *include* an eating/conversation area.

A multi-purpose area with separate furniture and lighting for each function.

Kitchen Noise

A kitchen area open to the family isn't always ideal, either. The disadvantage, usually, is to the family space.

Kitchens can be noisy. Conversing, listening to TV or music in the adjoining space can be difficult with kitchen talk, food preparation noises, and the dishwasher going.

Planning ahead will minimize conflict. Keep in mind that "sound-proofing" usually is not required, but rather sound reduction. An open kitchen can be effectively closed-off at certain times. For instance:

1. Opposed pocket doors will typically close an opening about six feet wide (see illustration).
2. Folding doors can stack up against a wall surface or recess into a pocket (see illustration).
3. Folding doors extending from a ceiling track to the counter top is another option.

Kitchen Odors

Odors from food prep and cooking are bound to permeate adjacent areas. Some odors are welcome and stimulate the appetite. Other odors don't have quite the same effect.

Solutions vary depending on where you shop or what catalogs come in the mail. There are herbs to steam, filters to absorb, and special candles to diffuse certain odors. Above all, after opening windows, have a good two-speed exhaust fan.

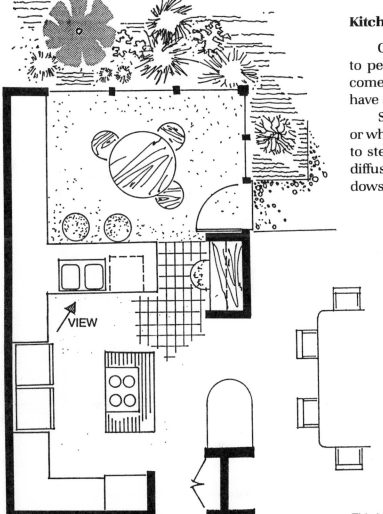

This kitchen interacts with breakfast, dining, and living areas beyond. Outside recreation is within view.

WHEN OPEN PLANNING IS REQUIRED

Home design to encourage interaction generally means some degree of open planning. Open planning has benefits beyond contact between cook/homemaker and people in other spaces.

Open planning usually means less maintenance. There are fewer walls, corners, and doors to clean. In addition, the general atmosphere might be a brighter, more cheerful, and spacious feeling.

A woman in Michigan makes a good case for open planning with this statement: "I work all day in an office. When I come home I like a feeling of space, and want to be able to talk with family."

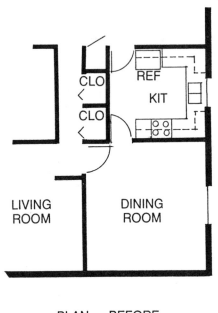

PLAN — BEFORE

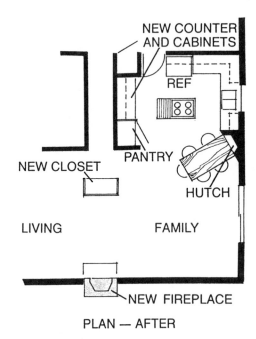

PLAN — AFTER

This renovation made better use of the available space and increased interaction between cook and family.

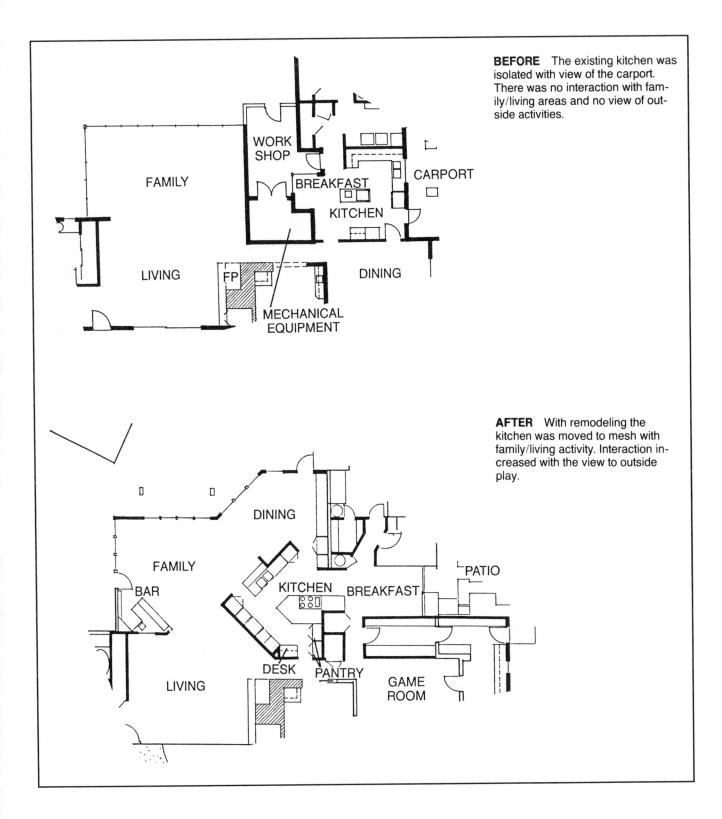

BEFORE   The existing kitchen was isolated with view of the carport. There was no interaction with family/living areas and no view of outside activities.

AFTER   With remodeling the kitchen was moved to mesh with family/living activity. Interaction increased with the view to outside play.

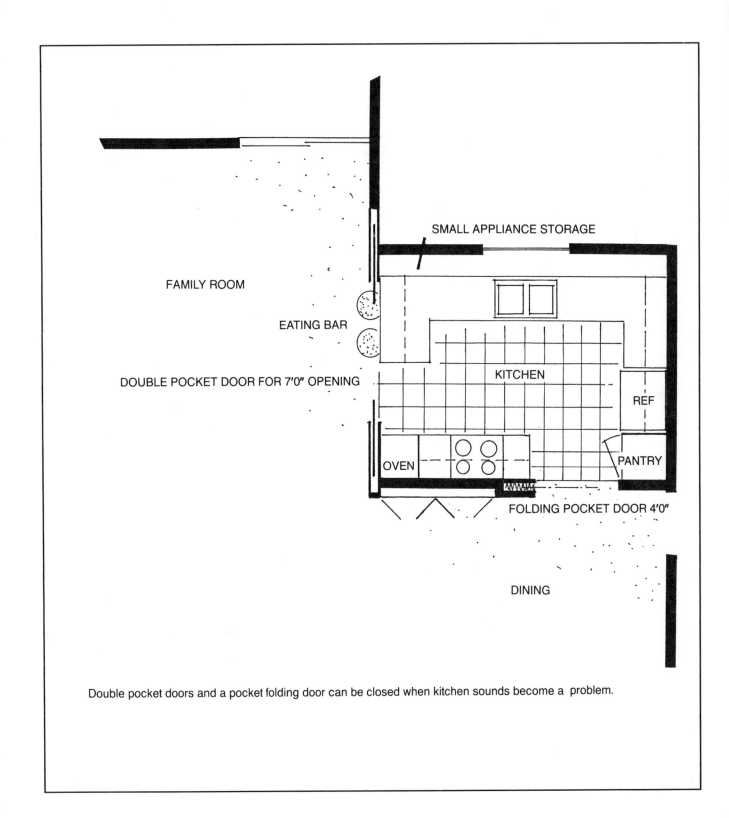

SMALL APPLIANCE STORAGE

FAMILY ROOM

EATING BAR

DOUBLE POCKET DOOR FOR 7'0" OPENING

KITCHEN

REF

OVEN

PANTRY

FOLDING POCKET DOOR 4'0"

DINING

Double pocket doors and a pocket folding door can be closed when kitchen sounds become a problem.

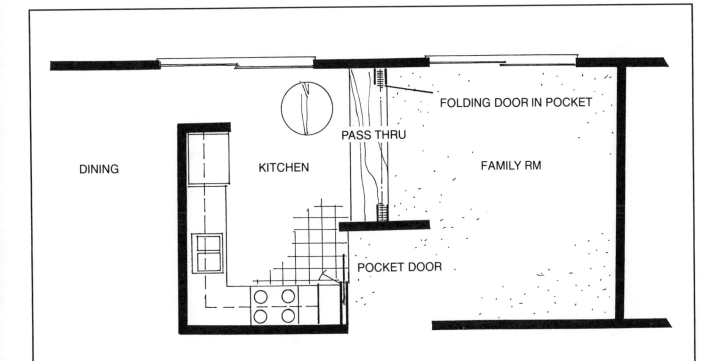

DINING

KITCHEN

PASS THRU

FOLDING DOOR IN POCKET

FAMILY RM

POCKET DOOR

Pocket door and folding doors above pass-through counter will reduce kitchen noise when needed.

3
Private —
Quiet Places

Asked what feature she would most like to have, an Arizona woman said, "Privacy is paramount to a woman with a job. A place to read and to think, with some beauty, is a must."

I would add that it's also important to a woman who does not have an outside job, but maybe has a house full of kids.

Remember also that *all* family members benefit from their own "private place." In fact, yours will work better if each person has an area that is strictly personal.

CUSTOM DESIGN FOR FAMILY NEEDS

Customizing home design for the occupants definitely carries into the planning of quiet places. For some, the need for privacy and quiet is not important. The lifestyles of many, however, insist on it. A woman in Pennsylvania put it this way: "Entertaining or cook-outs are the only times the whole family does much interacting — we usually pursue individual activities and appreciate privacy and quiet."

Inside Privacy — Planned and Found

An Arizona woman told me what she looked for in a house: "Generally, an open airy environment throughout the house with lots of natural light, while encouraging privacy."

That sounds like a nice place to me. To achieve it, however, requires that you specifically define those desires early. After all, open planning and private spaces don't naturally go together.

Set the need for private spaces in the *planning stage* of a new home or renovation. Give your designer an idea about the type of private spaces you would like to have. Then be sure they are included in a design featuring the "airy environment" of open planning.

A closed-off room for your private space usually is best. But if that can't be done, find options within other spaces. What is needed, by most, is that the space be *yours*. If it's only a corner, it still can have your favorite chair, a table, plants, artwork you've chosen, a source for your own music, etc.

Stress Goes Away

Much has been written about the benefit of water for reducing stress. Most of us can't have full-blown waterfalls in the living room, but small-scale effects are possible. We can have small fountains and aquariums. Or, even without actual water, it's relaxing to enjoy the visual effect with a painting or photograph.

The color scheme in your private space will influence its benefit to you. Consider the prime purpose of the space. Choose from the range of your favorite colors to best enhance the sense of

A window seat makes a nice private place.

A small window seat with storage underneath, in a child's room.

well being. Combine good light quality with your color scheme to ensure a balanced atmosphere for your space.

LOCATIONS

The purpose of a quiet place is to calm, refresh, and restore your senses. Naturally, the highest degree of "quiet privacy" comes in a closed-off room, but many other locations offer possibilities.

The Alcove

This space could be a private corner, niche, nook, cubicle, a bay window, or even a window seat in a stair landing. There are many possibilities.

The Open Study

This area can be the short end of an "L" shaped space. An asset to this arrangement is the ability to close it off visually. A folding door works well for that purpose.

Loft

This space comes in many flavors. It can occur anywhere, even in a small home or condo. A characteristic of the loft is that it allows a degree of privacy without being isolated.

Your Own Desk in a Multi-Purpose Space

There are many ways to achieve this, making it your own private part of the room. A partial screening of the area helps increase the sense of privacy. File cabinets or book shelves can serve double duty to provide that effect.

Arrangement of Space and Furniture

The advantage of planning private space *before* construction becomes evident here. Variation in floor elevation or ceiling height helps give the effect of a separate space within a space. In addition, lighting design, floor finish, and furniture layout work to create individual areas.

The Bath

If the closed-off space is only temporarily yours, it's good if it happens to be in a tub of hot water.

A quiet time in the bath is often the *only* private time in a busy life. It is, therefore, important that the factors of good design — lighting, colors, etc. — are in place.

Off the Bedroom

An area off the bedroom, used as an office or for reading, is a natural private place. You may want to make it a sun-space or include bookshelves and a fireplace. Other amenities for this area might be a small wet bar, refrigerator, and microwave. TV, VCR, and stereo complete the scene making it a home away from home, within the home.

Outside Privacy

At certain times of the day, under a special tree, near moving water, sitting on a deck catching the sun — any of these will offer private, quiet moments.

A Utah woman told me: "I enjoy having an outdoor area to go to. It's important for me to have this area as private and as beautiful as the space allows."

Increase the sense of privacy by adding small sections of wall, or landscaping such as boulders, shrubs, or earth mounds.

Landscaping and Design

We are not talking here about walking through the woods to a beautiful glen, or sitting on a flat rock beside your own private pond. That is fine, but not possible for most of us living on an average

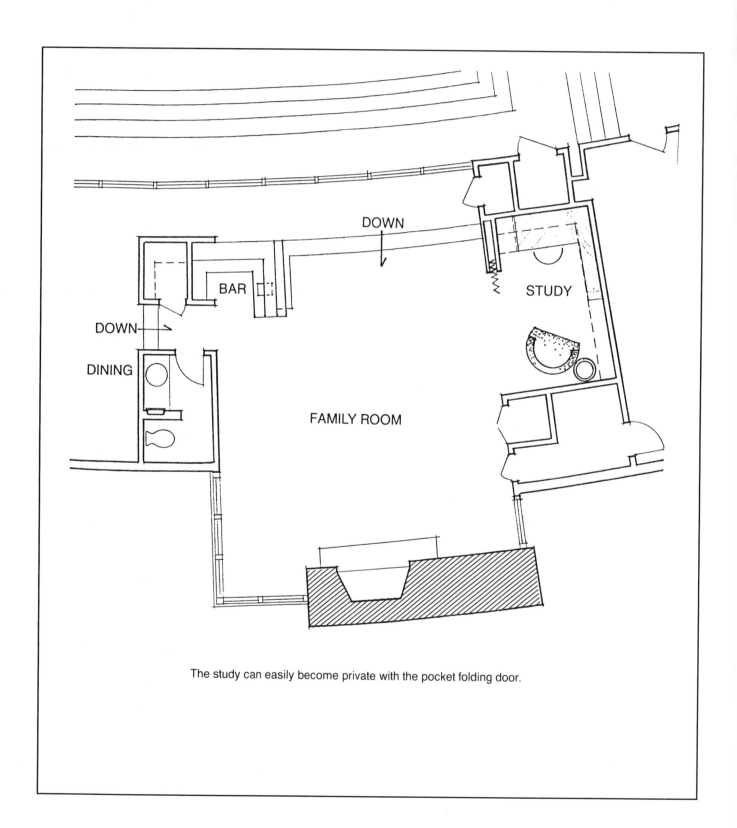

The study can easily become private with the pocket folding door.

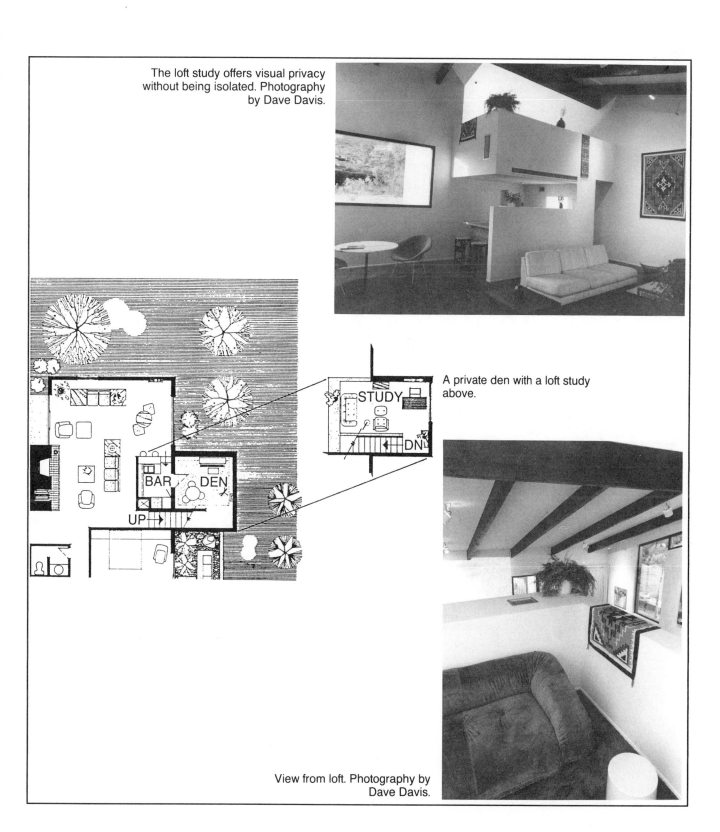

The loft study offers visual privacy without being isolated. Photography by Dave Davis.

A private den with a loft study above.

View from loft. Photography by Dave Davis.

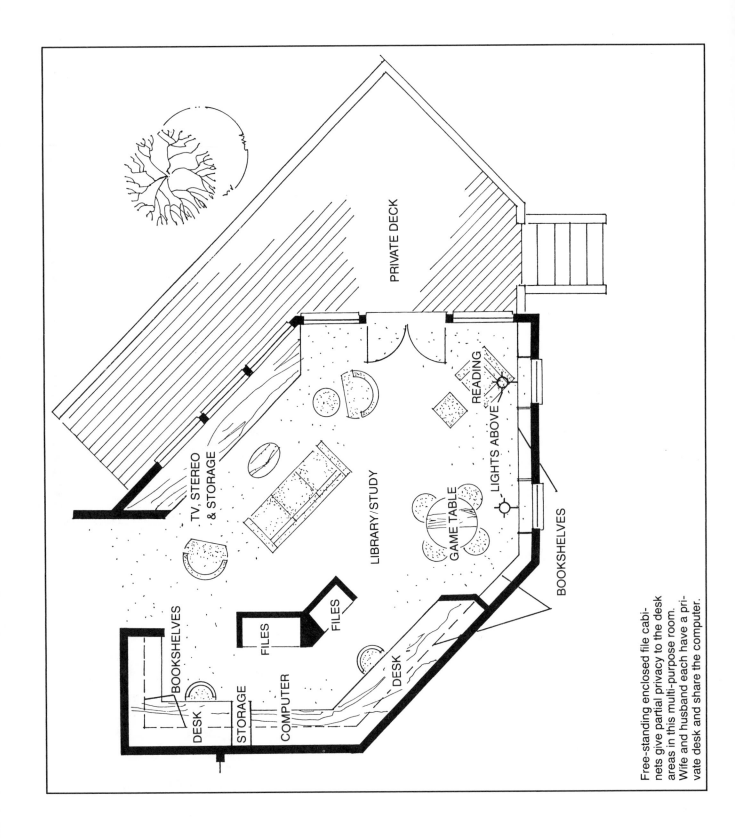

PRIVATE DECK

TV, STEREO & STORAGE

LIBRARY/STUDY

READING

LIGHTS ABOVE

GAME TABLE

BOOKSHELVES

BOOKSHELVES

FILES

FILES

DESK

STORAGE

COMPUTER

DESK

Free-standing enclosed file cabinets give partial privacy to the desk areas in this multi-purpose room. Wife and husband each have a private desk and share the computer.

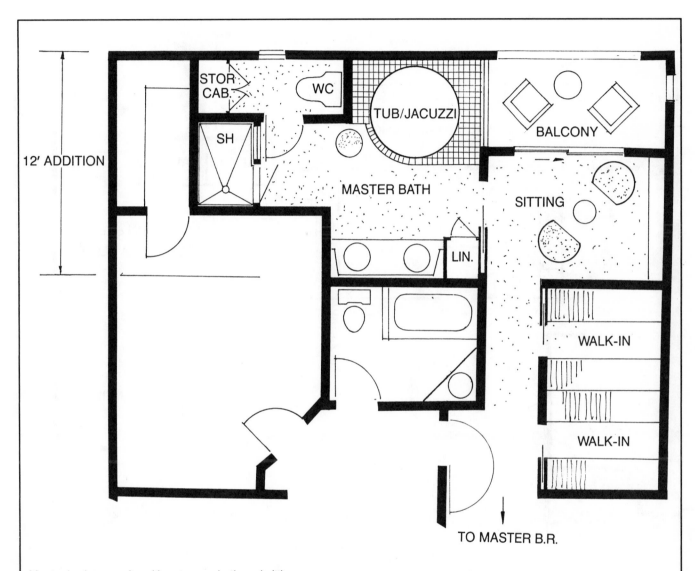

12′ ADDITION

STOR. CAB.

WC

SH

TUB/JACUZZI

BALCONY

MASTER BATH

SITTING

LIN.

WALK-IN

WALK-IN

TO MASTER B.R.

Master bedroom suite with get-away bath and sitting areas.

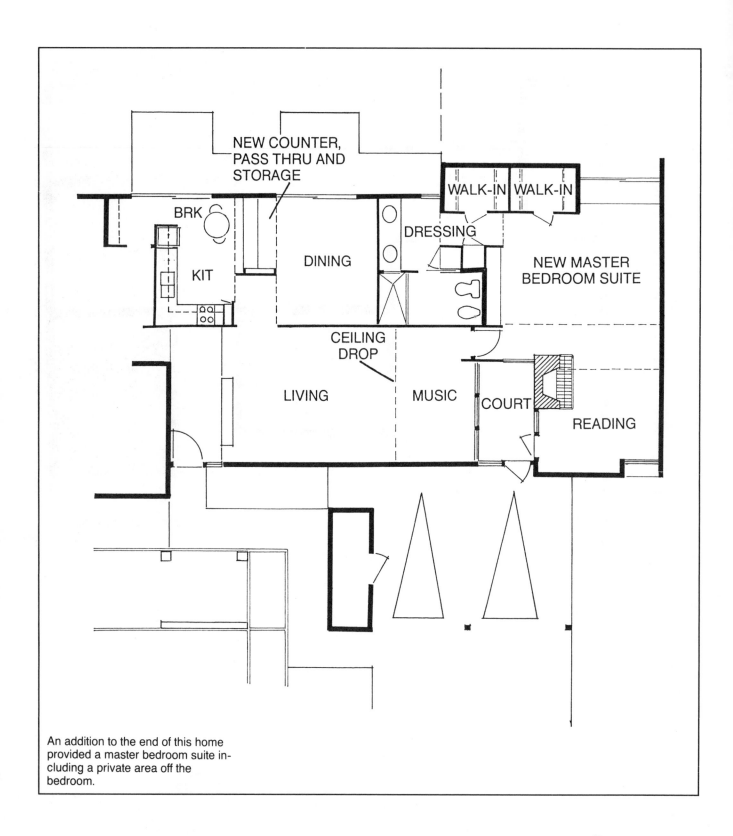

NEW COUNTER,
PASS THRU AND
STORAGE

BRK

WALK-IN WALK-IN

DRESSING

DINING

KIT

NEW MASTER
BEDROOM SUITE

CEILING
DROP

LIVING

MUSIC

COURT

READING

An addition to the end of this home
provided a master bedroom suite including a private area off the
bedroom.

A quiet personal space for reading.

A sunken area as part of a large space provides a feeling of privacy.

A deck for quiet conversation with a view.

building lot. What is required is being inventive in the relatively small areas outside our homes.

The illustrations shown here tell the story of two homes whose outside spaces were redone.

The illusion of water created with the precise placement of little stones or raked sand are just two of the subtle effects in a traditional Japanese garden. This kind of magic can happen in a very small space. You don't need acreage to create your outdoor "quiet place."

The aesthetic pleasure of good landscaping and the enjoyment of quiet places go hand in hand. Whether renovating or building new, make exterior design, and complete landscaping part of your budget.

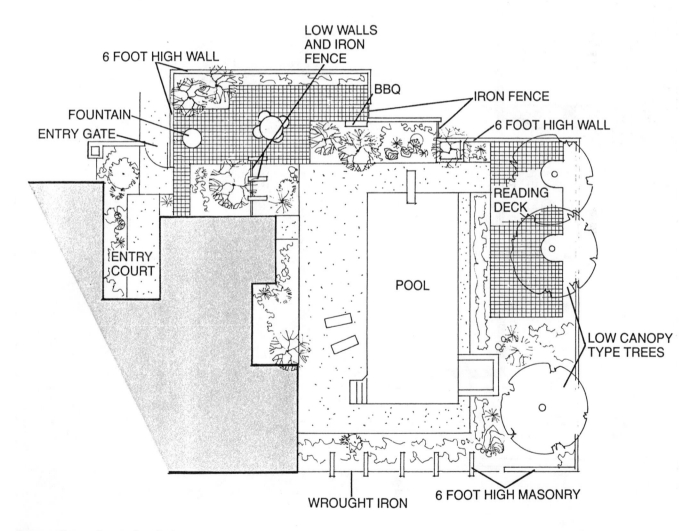

Surrounding walls create private areas that don't feel closed in.

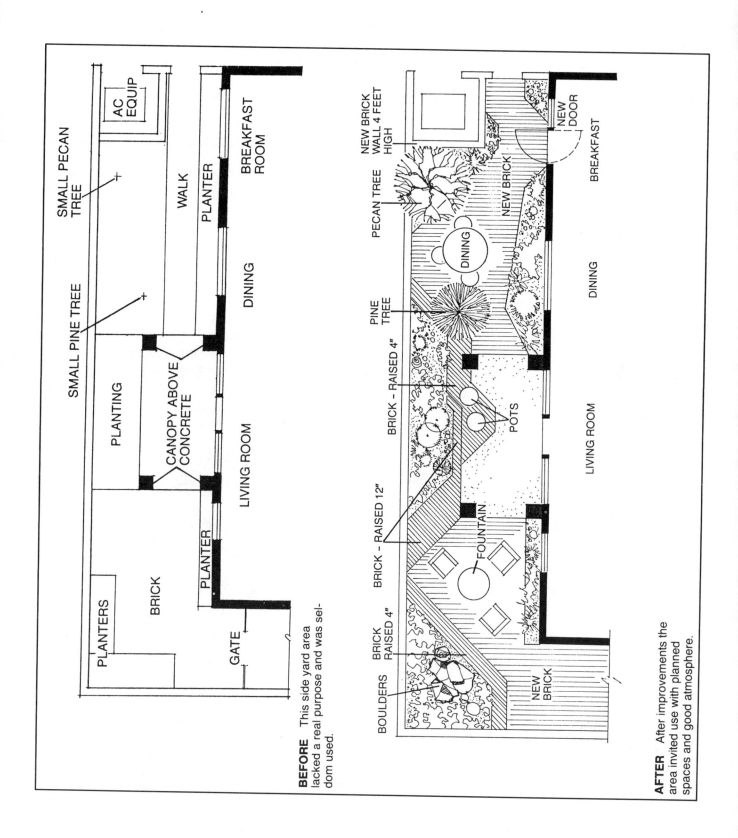

BEFORE This side yard area lacked a real purpose and was seldom used.

(Labels in BEFORE plan:) SMALL PECAN TREE · AC EQUIP · SMALL PINE TREE · WALK · PLANTER · BREAKFAST ROOM · DINING · PLANTING · CANOPY ABOVE CONCRETE · LIVING ROOM · PLANTERS · BRICK · PLANTER · GATE

AFTER After improvements the area invited use with planned spaces and good atmosphere.

(Labels in AFTER plan:) NEW BRICK WALL 4 FEET HIGH · NEW DOOR · PECAN TREE · NEW BRICK · DINING · BREAKFAST · PINE TREE · BRICK – RAISED 4" · POTS · DINING · BRICK – RAISED 12" · FOUNTAIN · LIVING ROOM · BRICK RAISED 4" · BOULDERS · NEW BRICK

4
Convenience and Kitchen Design

Convenience is defined as "anything that adds to one's comfort or saves work." Maximum convenience is a goal for every busy woman's home. A woman in Arizona said: "With over fifty percent of the women in the work force, it's critical that the house be as efficient as today's offices."

Every woman, with or without an outside job, should have optimum household convenience. It's an obtainable goal. Let's consider the busiest of all places, the kitchen.

KITCHEN DESIGN

When answering the question, "What special convenience or feature do you wish you had?" a Utah woman said: "A super plan for an efficient kitchen."

Knowing *how* to design an efficient kitchen isn't enough. Here is another part of the picture, from a woman in Colorado: " . . . women generally accept whatever kitchen layout is offered to them without actually thinking about how they function in a kitchen." Sadly, what she said happens all too often.

Get it Right the First Time

When building a new house there is little excuse for a poor kitchen. That is not to say there is no *reason* for it. There are many reasons for kitch-

ens being inefficient, small, poorly lighted, short of storage, etc. Responsibility, however, is another matter. You, the homemaker, must GET INVOLVED.

Your new kitchen should meet *your* specifications. You work there. The layout should suit *you*. Have counters convenient for your work habits, and storage where you need it most. Have lighting designed to make your work easier, and appliances that you prefer, in colors to suit your taste. And so it goes . . . But it won't happen by accident. INSIST ON IT!

FAMILY COOPERATION

Some kitchen complaints relate to factors other than design. For instance, one woman in Texas said: "Right now, everything is dropped on my counter. I have to clean up before I even attempt dinner." While that can relate to lack of space, cooperation from others sure helps.

Another woman said she "must go through dining room and kitchen to get to the family room." Well, that design flaw should be treated as a priority remodeling job!

THE WORK AREA

Kitchen convenience begins in the "work area." Planning the *work area* is the most important part of efficient kitchen design. Key elements are:

(1) the work triangle; (2) storage; (3) pantry; (4) type and location of appliances; (5) lighting. Let's take them one at a time.

THE WORK TRIANGLE

There isn't one magic layout — many work well. In each layout, however, the sink, cook top, and refrigerator will form a triangle. The three sides of an efficient triangle generally total between fourteen and twenty feet. (There are rare exceptions, one being a one-counter kitchen, with all functions lined up along one wall.)

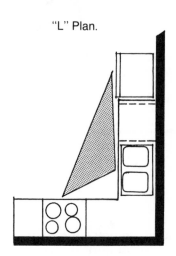

"L" Plan.

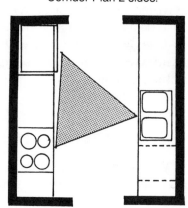

Corridor Plan 2 sides.

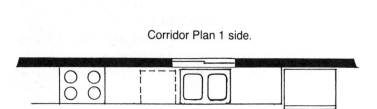

Corridor Plan 1 side.

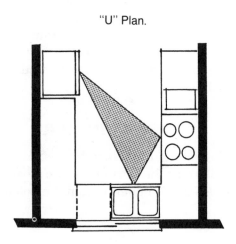

"U" Plan.

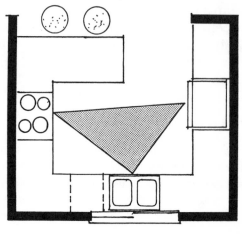

"U" Plan with peninsula.

An efficient layout for you is the one that best suits *your* methods of preparation, cooking/baking, and clean-up. Many women are very definite about which plan is best. For instance, a retired working woman in Washington said, "From long years of cooking and baking in many kitchens, a U-shaped, not too large, kitchen is the best for a homemaker."

KITCHEN STORAGE

Lack of convenient storage is the most common kitchen complaint I have received. And it's no wonder!

Poor storage means that: (1) counters are permanently cluttered; (2) cleaning takes longer; (3) over-stuffed cabinets make it hard to get things in and out; (4) more dishes and glasses are broken; (5) things used in the kitchen must be stored elsewhere; (6) time-saving appliances are not acquired due to lack of space; (7) frustration is guaranteed.

Planning a New Kitchen

Careful planning is the secret to good storage. (See Planning Considerations in Kitchen Design, Item 13.) Work out your kitchen on paper. As you plan, imagine yourself working in the space.

It's easy to overlook space needed for some items, like small appliances. Write *down* storage needs as you think of them. Keep a check list file. A few examples are listed below to direct your thinking.

Start answering questions like these and you will soon be into real planning:

1. What storage should be near sink?
2. What storage should be near cook top or oven?
3. What storage should be near the serving or eating areas?
4. Where do you want dishes, glassware, silver, utensils, etc.?
5. How will you store pots and pans?
6. Will you need a place for a drinking fountain or storing bottled water and dispenser?

7. What storage is needed for special shapes, such as large trays and bowls, tall glassware, portable appliances, etc.?

Adding Convenient Storage when Remodeling

It's usually possible to create additional storage and improve existing storage without enlarging your kitchen.

To devise the most effective use of all enclosed spaces, look for wasted space and put it to use.

Shallow cabinets (about 10″ deep) are an efficient use of space for most pantry items.

The Pantry

Pantry space is seldom planned well. Usually, the pantry is given whatever space is left over.

Locate the pantry to best serve cooking and eating habits. Plan the size, arrangement, and shelving depth for items you normally store.

More than one location may be best — and storage doesn't have to be in cabinets or closets. Drawers, glide-out shelves, bins, or lazy susans are handy for part of your stock — located where it's used. Shallow closets (about 10" deep) are an efficient use of space for most pantry items.

A lazy susan provides convenient storage in the corner.

A deep drawer is convenient pantry storage for certain items like cereal boxes.

LIGHTING

Natural daylight opens and brightens up a kitchen space. Get it where you can — from above or even from adjacent rooms.

In the right orientation and climate, use as many windows as space allows. Generally, that isn't a lot because economy of space dictates that walls contain cabinets and appliances. Some artificial light usually is needed, even during the day.

Some women prefer high intensity light in work areas only. Others want well distributed light throughout the kitchen.

For overall light quality, I prefer a well designed, recessed, fluorescent-tube luminous ceiling. It can be double switched for added convenience. Double switching saves energy. One switch provides soft lighting and, when needed, the second switch will energize more tubes and provide task-quality lighting throughout the kitchen. See the chapter on Light for illustrations.

Skylights are an option to add daylight, cheer up the space, and improve function. In hot climates, locate skylights away from intense sun exposure. It's no fun to have bright light that overheats a space already warm from appliances and cooking.

COMMUNICATION FOR CONVENIENCE

When did you last prepare a meal only to discover everyone scattered throughout the house when it was ready? Probably last night.

A good intercom system saves time and a lot of steps. It needn't be elaborate. Use a simple call system, with master control in the kitchen and speakers, for receiving/answering, in key areas. Typical speaker locations are bedrooms, basement, workshop, patio, and other spaces likely to contain people.

Equipment is available that will operate through the electrical wiring system in your existing home. Cost is moderate. Always be certain that equipment you buy is UL approved, and is installed

Combination desk and eating counter with cookbook library and wall-mounted phone. Efficiency and convenience continue with stool storage in the dead corner.

in accordance with the manufacturer's instructions.

KITCHEN LIBRARY

Your cooking library belongs in the kitchen. Plan the space for book shelving, reading, writing, sorting recipes, etc.

Desk space in the area is another good option, combined with the library. A *telephone* in the kitchen is a must. If not at the desk, a wall phone with long cord works well and is one item less to move and clean around.

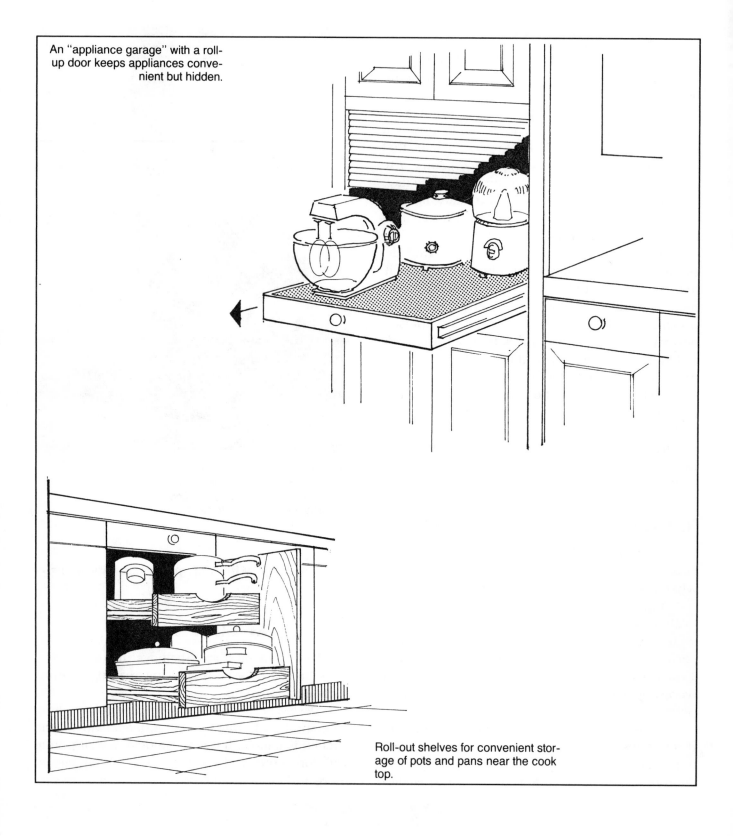

An "appliance garage" with a roll-up door keeps appliances convenient but hidden.

Roll-out shelves for convenient storage of pots and pans near the cook top.

APPLIANCES

Choice and location of large appliances determine the work triangle mentioned earlier. About forty percent of your time is spent at the sink. Refrigerator, stove, and dishwasher naturally relate to that location. A microwave, for some women, should also be located in the work center. Depending on your methods, regular ovens may be placed outside the work triangle.

An *ice maker* in the refrigerator should be standard equipment for a busy woman.

A garbage *disposal* is convenient. A good one will last many years, save you time, and decrease mess and odor. Just remember that it can also chew up fingers. *Never* put your hand inside it to dislodge something, even when it's off.

I am often asked if a garbage disposal is okay to use with a septic system. In my experience, if you have a good system and use common sense about what to put in the disposal, it won't be a problem. However, no general rule covers all situations. Check it out with your local experts.

A *trash compactor* is convenient as well, although it gets mixed reviews as a necessary time/labor saving feature. Also, I don't like to see them installed in a house with small children present.

Small Appliances

The type, number, and location of small appliances is a very personal matter. Some of the finest cooks use few small appliances, while others are gadget happy. One thing is sure, however, they all take space.

Kitchen storage is *always* a problem. Don't acquire another small appliance unless you have a place to put it. Cluttering the counter with "convenience" items will decrease convenience.

Consumer surveys are a standard source to check any appliance from refrigerator to can opener. Included should be tips on efficiency, storage, capacity, maintenance, and overall operation. It's a good starting point for appliance selection.

Convenient storage for kitchen and dining is shown here with built-in cabinets for china, silver, glassware, linens, and accessories. Note: It's also easy to clean.

PLANNING

In new construction, kitchen planning is relatively easy. In remodeling, we plan with existing conditions. Some of those existing items are plumbing and electrical systems, doors, and windows.

Weigh the Values

Usually, economy dictates that you work with existing conditions. However, don't get locked into the idea of keeping all fixtures and cabinets in the same place. Doing that, you can miss out on a better plan — one which may require only minor changes, but greatly increase convenience.

I am not suggesting you ignore the cost. But don't lose sight of the main objective — making your kitchen a more efficient and pleasant space.

Dining Spaces

Gracious and relaxed dining includes good atmosphere and convenience. Convenience in

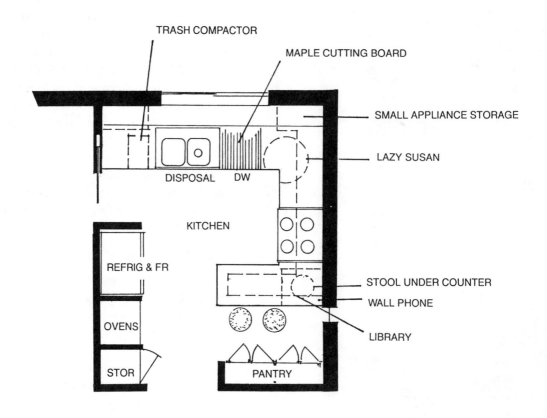

PLAN VIEW
(See cut-away view)

An efficient use of space for a kitchen with convenience.

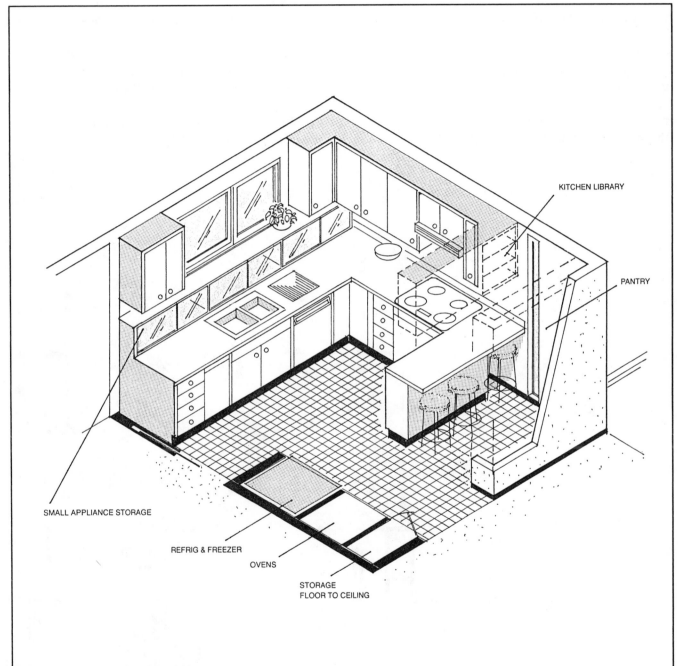

KITCHEN LIBRARY

PANTRY

SMALL APPLIANCE STORAGE

REFRIG & FREEZER

OVENS

STORAGE
FLOOR TO CEILING

CUT-AWAY VIEW

This compact kitchen was designed
for efficiency and convenience.

dining includes its proximity to the kitchen. Satisfy the dining-kitchen relationship. Then relate the dining area to other spaces, and to the outside if possible.

Casual dining is another matter. It's seldom more convenient than when it happens right in the kitchen. In fact, a cozy kitchen eating area becomes host to a lot of convenient living. While you are thinking about it, consider the TV.

When asked if she watched TV while eating,

one woman said, "Yes, but I wish I didn't." Others said, "No, that's family time." And, "Yes, since the children are grown."

My survey suggests that a large number of us often watch TV while eating — probably a majority. If *you* do, it's time to face reality. Design an area for the purpose. Whether it's in, adjacent to, or just near the kitchen, make it comfortable as well as convenient.

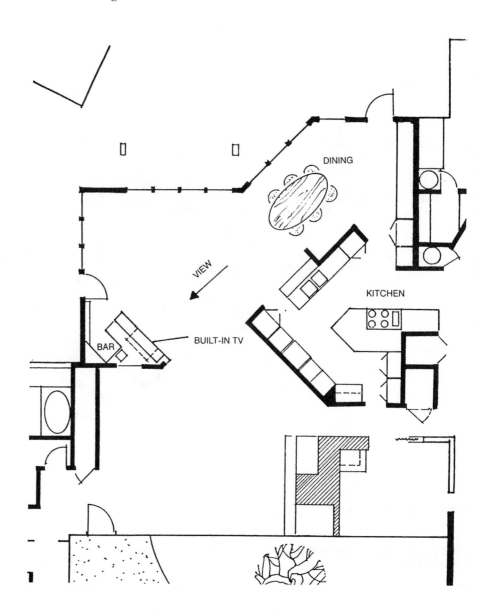

This family wanted the TV in view from the dining table.

PLANNING CONSIDERATIONS IN KITCHEN DESIGN

Below is a list of planning considerations. Consider the items, and add or delete as you wish. Then use it as a check list when building new or remodeling.

1. Total counter space needed:
   (a) If remodeling, do you need all the existing counter? What isn't well used could be converted to a storage cabinet extending from floor to ceiling.
   (b) At the sink, 18″ to 36″ is required on each side. The amount depends on your work methods. Have at least 36″ on one side.
   (c) At the cook top, have 24″ minimum on one side. Provide a heat-resistant insert for hot pots.
   (d) At the refrigerator, a counter 18″ to 24″ at the handle side is the minimum for food on its way in or out.
   (e) For food preparation (mixing, baking), combine in one counter space or two separate spaces — whatever your preference. Have 48″ minimum with the combined use.
   (f) A serving counter is handy. Located between the work triangle and dining area, it can serve double duty as eating or bar counter.
   (g) Do you want an eating counter?
   (h) Will you have a wet bar elsewhere? (Relates to storage for beer, wine, liquor, soft drinks, ice, etc.)
   Note: Overall, you need *adequate* counter space, not excessive counter space.

2. How many people work in food preparation? (Relates to size and arrangement of work area.)

3. Discuss cooking habits and preferences.
   (a) Be honest. Do you like to cook or is it a required chore? (Relates to things like pantry, freezer size, microwave and oven location, and all appliances.)

4. Family eating habits:
   (a) Where do you like to eat breakfast? Lunch? Dinner? What space is needed?
   (b) Do you want an eating area in the kitchen?
   (c) Does the family eat all meals together?

5. What kind of cook are you? Do you need:
   (a) extra storage for ingredients?
   (b) more counter for mixing and preparation?

6. Does the family gather in the kitchen during meal preparation? (Relates to space near the work triangle for the non-workers.)

7. Does traffic route through the kitchen going to storage for beer, wine, liquor, soft drinks, ice, etc.?

8. What is the best counter height for you? The usual height is 36″. Dishwashers, trash compactors and full range units are made to fit under or flush with a 36″ counter. If you like to prepare food at a different height, change the counter height in the prep area. If below 36″, remember that appliances may not fit under that counter.

9. Do you entertain often? Formally or casually? (Relates to serving counter and storage space.)

10. Do you need cookbook shelving? Desk space?

11. Where do you want the telephone?

12. What is the desired access between kitchen and dining, or kitchen and family areas?

13. Think about general storage. For example:
    (a) Optimum use of all cabinet space relates to type of drawers, shelving, and their locations.
    (b) Do you need spaces for special items, such as knives, trays, large pots, etc.?
    (c) Check your glassware, silver, portable appliances, etc., for storage needs.
    (d) Check needs for linens, paper, plastic wrap, foil, etc.
    (e) Provide storage near the cook top for cooking tools, pots, pans, skillets, etc.

14. Review pantry requirements. Do you store bulk items i.e., pet food, as well as cans, boxes, and bags?

15. What is your oven use? (Relates to location, type, and quantity.)

16. Do you want a microwave or other alternate cooking device?

17. What kind of lighting do you like?

18. Do you want an island? The island has benefits. It adds efficiency to certain layouts, and the look itself is a feature. However, the kitchen must be larger than average to include it. I feel you need four feet minimum between the island and nearest counter or appliance. Although many get by with less, it can get crowded with two people working, or when doors, drawers, or appliances (i.e., dishwasher) are opened.

19. The sink is the most used piece of equipment in the kitchen. Its location is key to a good layout.

20. Locate the cook top near the sink. It's the most heavily used leg in the work triangle.

21. How should the kitchen relate visually, audibly, and functionally to other spaces? For example, if rooms are small, consider opening up part of the kitchen to dining or family areas.

22. What have you always wanted in your kitchen? Add it to this list!

A telescoping pull-out table with
drop-down legs for extra space
when preparing meals or serving.

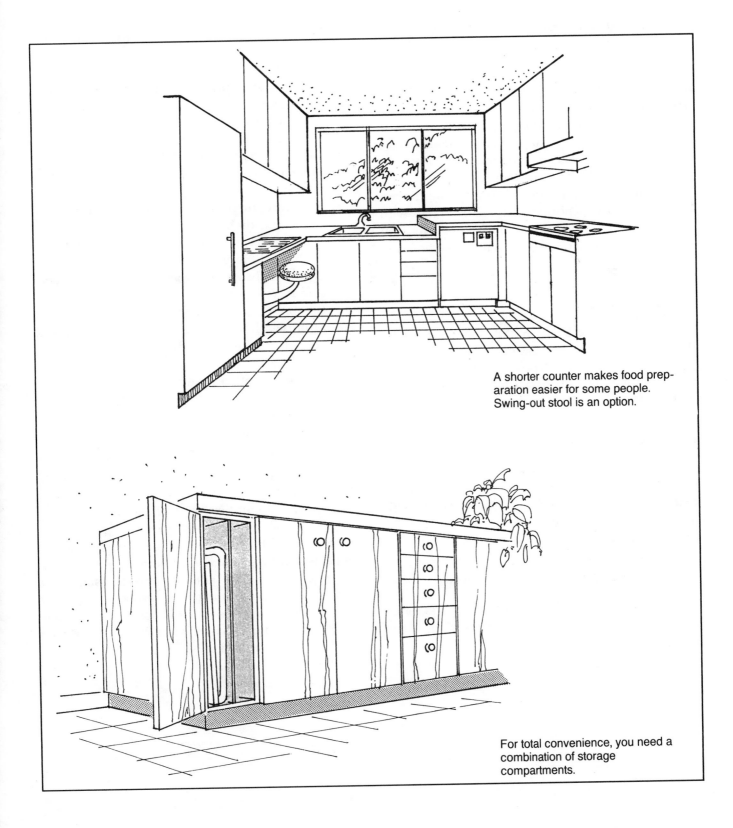

A shorter counter makes food preparation easier for some people. Swing-out stool is an option.

For total convenience, you need a combination of storage compartments.

CONVENIENCE EVOLUTION

In the past fifty years, "home building" has evolved to make life easier for the homemaker. We have better lighting, easier to clean floors and windows, garages attached to the house, and efficient, easy-to-use heating and cooling systems.

However, the giant steps for convenience have come in product design, such as appliances and packaged ready-to-heat/eat meals.

Home design, and subdivision housing, have a long way to go to produce ready-made homes with convenience in mind for you, the homemaker. You must keep insisting on higher quality pre-construction planning.

Be Wary and Wise

When looking at a "model home," don't be dazzled by the glint and glitter — *think how it will work for you.* Be aware of positive and negative factors in kitchen layouts, storage needs, laundry location, traffic flow, cleaning handicaps, etc.

Bedroom Convenience

There is every reason to expect convenience in bedroom, dressing, and closet areas. It's acquired with a good general layout and good storage built for these space. Check the Bedroom chapter for ideas and guidelines.

CONVENIENCE PRIORITIES

Keep a list of ideas to improve convenience and save time. You may want to include some of the following.

1. Storage throughout the house *where things are used.*
2. Laundry area near bedrooms.
3. Hamper and linen closets at each bath/bedroom area.
4. An efficient kitchen work area.
5. Increase kitchen storage to optimum.
6. Pantry storage *in* the kitchen.
7. Storage for small appliances where you use them.
8. An intercom/paging system with master control in the kitchen.
9. If necessary, customize counter, cabinet, and shelf height to your size.
10. Locate lighting and power outlets for convenience.
11. Customize switching for built-in lighting.
12. Multiple phones in a large house. At least one at each level in a multi-level house. (Save that mad dash, and increase safety.) A portable phone is another option, if you want to carry it around.
13. Don't overfurnish.
14. Study/improve the traffic flow.
15. A central vacuum system.

I will end this chapter on convenience with comments from an Arizona working woman who was musing about her future dream work space.

"I would like my own garage type of room where I could have an ironing board, washer, dryer, sinks for soaking, a sewing machine, plus an area for repotting plants and an area for starting a garden. As I hate ironing, it would be nice to have a TV to watch and also an area for exercise equipment. The room also needs lots of concealed storage, closet space, and to be airy and easy to clean."

5
Make Housecleaning Easy

To quote a woman in Michigan: "All women want to spend less time cleaning and increase quality time at home. . . ." She should have added — AND WE CAN DO IT.

I don't pretend to be a cleaning expert and this chapter won't give you all the ins and outs of *how* to clean. But I will give you ideas to help you *avoid the need to clean*.

Entire books have been written about how to clean. A popular one is *Do I Dust or Vacuum First* by Don Aslett.

SEAL THOSE CRACKS

Every house has dust filtering in somewhere. Many practically invite dust. The obvious places to check first: under, around, and above all windows and doors. Search out cracks everywhere, and seal, fill, plug, and insulate.

DESIGN — OPEN AND CLOSED PLANNING

In particular, the chapters on Convenience and Interaction discuss the benefits derived from either open or closed planning. But how does design and planning affect the *cleanability* of your home?

Open Planning

The design of your home definitely affects housecleaning needs. One design change occurring in newer housing has made housecleaning easier — the open plan. Open planning simply means space flowing freely, through wider openings, without doors, from one function to another.

Open planning means fewer walls, corners, doors, hardware, trim, and base material to clean. There is less secondary space to clean, like hallways.

Open planning results in "borrowed" light flowing from one space to another. Therefore, you will have fewer lamps or light fixtures, windows, and skylights to maintain.

There are pitfalls with open planning that you should be aware of. Openness can give the illusion of more space than there really is. An inherent danger with open planning, therefore, is the temptation to build or buy a house that is actually too small for your needs.

The result is permanent clutter and easy cleaning is *impossible* with clutter. When looking at

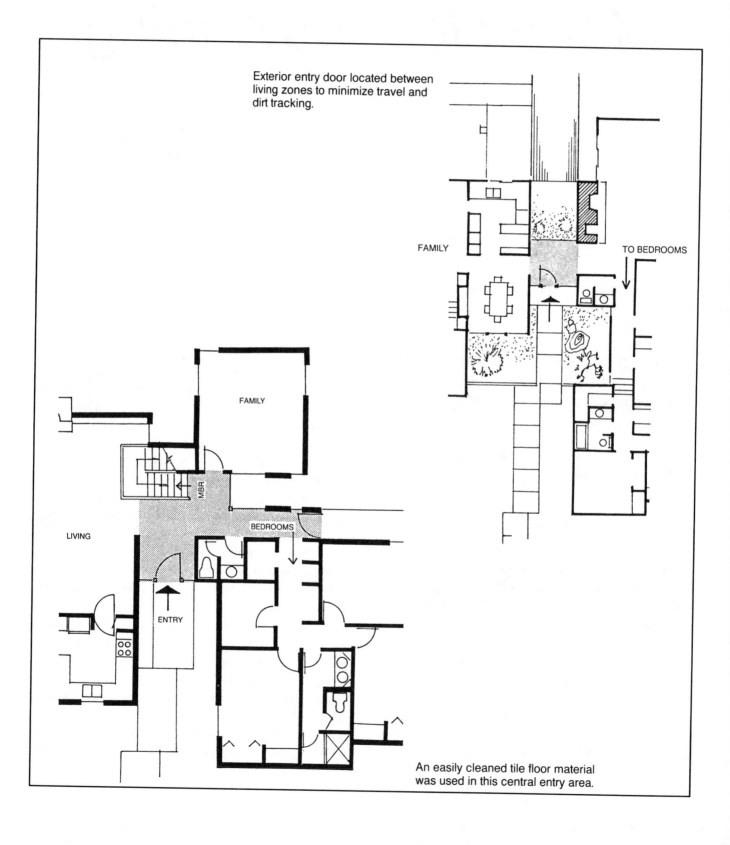

Exterior entry door located between living zones to minimize travel and dirt tracking.

FAMILY

TO BEDROOMS

FAMILY

MBR

BEDROOMS

LIVING

ENTRY

An easily cleaned tile floor material was used in this central entry area.

an open plan, carefully weigh total *space* against your lifestyle, furnishings, size of family, and storage needs.

STORAGE

A Michigan woman told me, "Every person needs good storage as it promotes order and neatness and helps eliminate lots of time-consuming work (dusting, cleaning, etc.)." I could not have said it better.

Ironically, ample storage is rare. In fact, there is seldom enough storage for the cleaning items themselves. Sometimes storage for cleaning supplies is located far from where you do the work.

Anti-clutter

Poor storage promotes clutter. Clutter is irritating. Increase storage, reduce irritation. Logic prevails.

Some of the happiest comments I have heard come from women with good storage facilities. Those lucky few say their homes are easier to clean and more fun to live in.

The chapter on Storage explores this subject in detail.

OTHER FACTORS

One Story is Easier

When you think about cleaning everything from floors and stairs to woodwork and windows, one-story living is the easiest to maintain.

The only cleaning advantage I see with a second floor is the possibility of cleaning it less often. Even then, to save time and labor, keep duplicate cleaning equipment on each floor.

Limit the Open Plan

Certain closed *spaces* are needed to enhance cleanability. Most homes have closed bedrooms, utility, and storage areas — and with good reason. Bedroom privacy is desirable. Closed-off utility, hobby, and laundry areas tend to keep the mess in one area.

And remember to locate the laundry where it should be — in the bedroom wing — so your clothes-cleaning steps are minimized.

Check the Traffic

Traffic flow greatly affects cleaning and maintenance. Tracking dirt through one area to get to another is kept to a minimum with good planning. Exterior doors can be located between zones or different functions to minimize traffic.

Provide an Entry

Bringing dirt from the front door directly onto the living room carpet is no more fun than mud from the back yard into the kitchen. Provide an entry way with a hard surface floor material (see illustrations).

Pet Control

Pet access in and out of the house requires planning to minimize mess. That subject is taken up in the chapter on Home Security.

WINDOWS

Window location determines the window covering required. A covering for a sliding glass door or window means something else to clean and maintain. With careful design, much of your glass won't need to be covered at all.

"Easier to clean windows" are high on the wish list for many women. Window cleaning is one of the least desired (sometimes totally dreaded!) housecleaning jobs. And yet, with the right design, glass cleaning is fairly quick and easy.

Window maintenance generally comes in two

forms — the glass and the frames. Easy glass cleaning relates to size and accessibility. Frame maintenance relates to the material and design.

Window Frames

In a new home, I try to use bronze-colored anodized aluminum window frames. They are almost maintenance free and will maintain a good appearance.

With wood frames, I try to keep the wood sections in a protected area. The reason for using wood usually is for the appearance of wood. There-fore, I normally apply a good stain and seal rather than paint. The south and west exposures, in most parts of the world, are hardest on wood and wood finishes. So be prepared to maintain those exposures more often.

A compromise for appearance and maintenance is metal-clad wood. It's a wood frame with an anodized aluminum casing over the outside portion of the wood. The inside surface is left as exposed wood. This construction is typical in a casement-type window and there are several good manufacturers. They are fairly expensive.

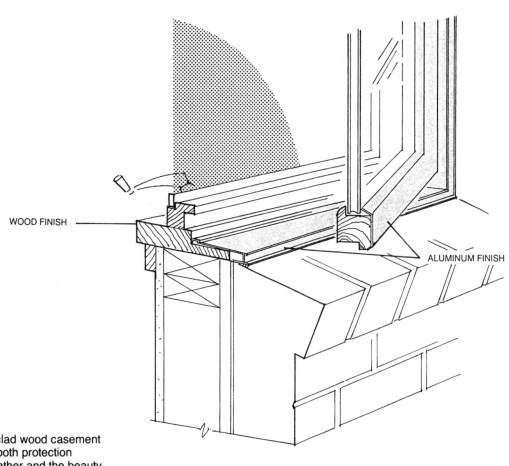

WOOD FINISH

ALUMINUM FINISH

An aluminum-clad wood casement window offers both protection against the weather and the beauty of wood inside the house.

Replacing Old Windows

Old homes, especially, may have wood-frame windows with many glass sections that are hard to operate, clean, and maintain. It's often possible to retro-fit new anodized aluminum windows to replace the wood. However, make such changes with care for the effect on your home's appearance.

Glass Maintenance — Reduce the Panes and Ease the Pain

Glass, one of our oldest building materials, is also one of the best. It does wonderful things for us. We get cheap light while enjoying views from the comfort of inside.

Glass should not be such a nuisance to maintain. Let's look at a few ways to ease the pain.

A common gripe — no outside cleaning access from inside — should eventually disappear.

Most operating windows — double hung, single hung, horizontal sliding, etc. — are now made for cleaning convenience. Window sections can be tilted or removed for inside cleaning. Look for this type of window when building a new home or remodeling an old one.

Glass size relates directly to ease of cleaning. Common sense says that one large single sheet is easier to clean than the same area broken up into sixteen separate panes of glass (a typical 4' x 4' opening).

Windows that open are limited in size, so large sheets of glass are usually fixed in place. They can be cleaned with a large squeegee inside and out. True, you have to go outside to clean, but a squeegee on a long pole sure beats hanging off a two-story ladder.

When considering a new home you may be tempted to go for windows with many panes of glass. Remember the cleaning! Each pane must be cleaned and wiped around the frame. And cleaning dozens of the little devils is compounded if they are on the second floor.

When house shopping or building, here, indeed, is a case where you must decide between the charm and the chore.

WINDOW COVERING

Any window covering adds extra maintenance, so deciding which one to use may be based on subjective rather than practical reasons. Overall home design is a strong factor. Here are some examples:

Drawstring drapes require less maintenance than blinds. Often, however, they cover part of the glass, even when open.

Vertical blinds don't get as dusty as horizontal blinds, but they can look somewhat commercial.

"Mini" blinds have more surfaces to clean than larger blinds, but let you see through the glass better.

Between-the-glass blinds are another option — expensive but effective. This is a window with a *very* mini-blind installed between two sheets of glass.

Reports from users tell me that some are more trouble-free than others. In some brands, the device to tilt the blinds becomes misaligned. Also, inside cleaning may sometimes be needed.

If you can afford to use between-the-glass blinds, check them first at the suppliers. Get names of homeowners who have used them for a couple of years.

No window covering: Where feasible, bare glass is the best solution. Where climate permits, I prefer to create a design that allows glass to remain uncovered. Some ways to accomplish this are:

1. Glass facing a walled or fenced-in private courtyard.
2. Glass so located (by design) that looking in from outside won't interfere with your privacy.
3. High glass — above eye level from outside.
4. Locate landscaping to shield windows from onlookers and the sun.
5. Ignore the whole thing and forget that anyone can look in.

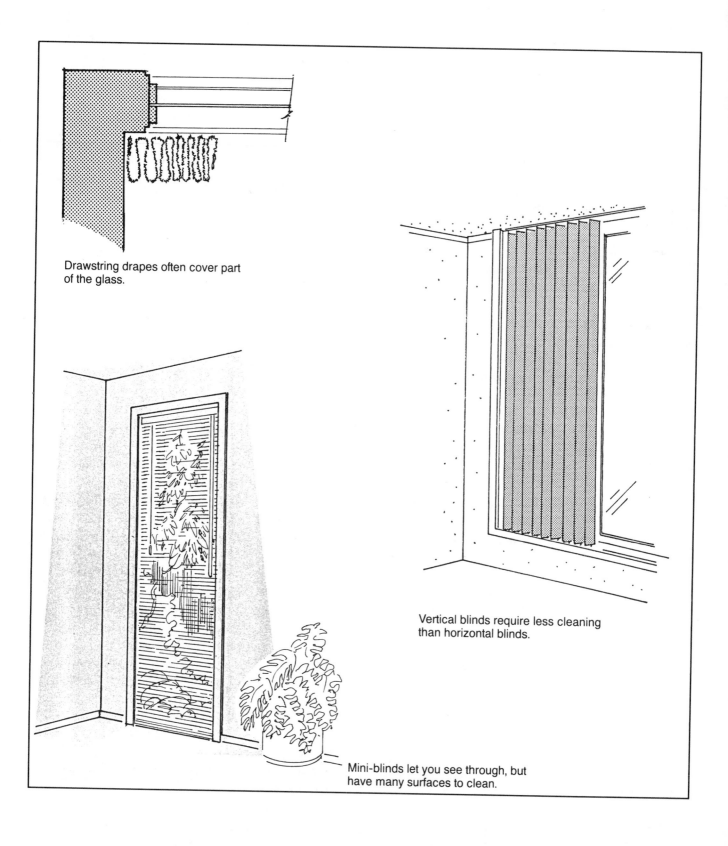

Drawstring drapes often cover part of the glass.

Vertical blinds require less cleaning than horizontal blinds.

Mini-blinds let you see through, but have many surfaces to clean.

No window covering is needed with the right combination of overhang, wall, landscaping, and orientation.

The kitchen relates to the outdoor breakfast patio.

Protected from the sun and outside
eyes, this large sheet of glass enliv-
ens the space and is easy to clean.

This north facing glass is easy to
clean and needs no covering.

Built-in bed and adjacent cabinets wall-to-wall. This built-to-the-floor smooth surface furniture promotes easy cleaning.

In many homes I have designed, the only glass covering required is for bedroom privacy or temperature control.

Sun control: Direct sun on unprotected glass means hot, bright sun inside. There are some options. Solar glass is nice, but has a limited effect. Reflecting glass is more effective, but can look tacky if poorly used. When used in a house, I prefer a minimum reflectance, 40-50%, and use it carefully, catering to the exterior appearance.

Future option: Science and manufacturing are sure to bring new glass options. One of those may be a double-glazed window that can be switched from clear to opaque with electromagnetic controls. The technology is nearly in place.

FURNISHINGS

What makes housecleaning easier? In answer to that question a woman who cleans houses for a living said, "Simple furnishings." I would add to that and say, "And not too many of them!"

Under-furnish rather than over-furnish. When you do this, interior spaces are not only easier to clean, they look better and cost less money!

Design

In furniture design, common sense is the guide. Fussy, over-detailed furniture is hard to clean. Short legs under a sofa, leaving an impossible to reach space underneath, create a cleaning problem.

For easier cleaning, consider these options: (1) Straight line, smooth surface furniture built to the floor is easy to clean; (2) Wall-hung pieces make it easy to clean the floor underneath; (3) Built-in furniture means even fewer places for dust to collect.

FLOOR FINISH

In custom construction, get the floor finish you *want*. Have a personal impact on future maintenance. Even in tract housing you should have floor finish choices. Assert yourself to get easy maintenance floors if you so wish.

When buying an older house, getting a low maintenance floor can be more difficult. However, the cost of changing a high maintenance floor finish is a good argument for lowering the purchase price by the same amount.

I have received many opinions about floors in response to the question, "What would make housecleaning easier?" Here are a few of them.

"One type of flooring throughout"
"No-wax flooring"
"All hardwood floors"
"Carpeting throughout"
"Stain-resistant carpets"
"Tile rather than carpet"
"Easy to clean flooring"

Well, nobody said we couldn't have different opinions. Let's talk about each of these. First, this comment from a Utah woman: "One type of flooring throughout." Surely, using the same equipment to clean all floors *could* be an advantage. However, no one material is the best for all areas or all types of use. One material throughout can simplify the *type* of cleaning required, but the *amount* and *quality* of cleaning varies greatly with traffic conditions.

By all means though, limit the number of times you *change* the finish flooring. Don't use three types of flooring in one space and then complain it's hard to maintain.

Carpet

"Carpeting throughout" was suggested. Let's look at some pros and cons.

Carpeting *is* the most popular flooring for living areas. It offers many colors and textures and has a feeling of warmth and comfort. The extensive price range and general good quality mean excellent value, hence its wide appeal.

On the down side, carpet is not the best in areas of heavy traffic. Don't use it where liquid or food spillage is likely. (Where carpet has been successfully used in kitchen or bath, it's where *control is possible* — that usually means no children.) Also, carpet can be a problem for those with allergies.

Note: Giant strides have been made in stain-resistant carpeting. Look for new products and new guarantees in this area.

A smooth surface, wall-hung dresser makes cleaning a snap.

Wood

"All hardwood floors" was another suggestion. That women disagree on the best floor indicates the problem with one material for all situations. Your habits, lifestyle, and the traffic patterns in your home all play a part. Wind, rain, snow, and soil conditions around your house influence the kind of mess that ends up on your floors.

Hardwood flooring comes *close* to being a material usable for all floors. Usable, however, doesn't always mean *good*. Hardwood floors can be beautiful, warm, cleanable, satisfying, and are one of my favorites. But they have limitations.

Areas subject to abuse in utility rooms, work areas, and entry ways should be a harder floor surface. Glazed ceramic tile is easy to maintain in those areas. More economically finished and sealed colored concrete will do the job.

Kitchens and bathrooms are not considered the best places for hardwood. While I have used oak flooring in kitchens with success, that "success" required a combination of caring and careful homeowners, a good urethane finish, and accepting the fact of eventual refinishing and possible future replacement if abused.

The trick is to seal wood on the outside to prevent liquid penetrating it. A hard urethane finish will increase wood's resistance to water and staining. Most chemical finishes of this type show scratch marks and may be glossy, but are long lasting. Check samples in a dealer showroom for gloss, slip resistance, color, cleanability, etc.

It's ironic that now, in the age of better floor finishing products, there are relatively fewer wood floors than fifty years ago. Of course, many other products are available, such as ceramic tile, vinyl, and better carpet fibers.

Noise

Reverberation from walking, talking, music, etc., increases with large areas of wood floor. Tempering the sound with area rugs will increase cleaning time and decrease safety. I prefer to leave wood floors uncovered and use carpet for sound absorption where you need it most.

Ceramic Tile

"Tile, rather than carpet," is preferred by some. Glazed ceramic tile is an excellent floor for long wear and easy care. In fact, it's about the only material that really qualifies as "no wax flooring." Grout for the joints comes in many colors. Medium-toned colors are easiest to maintain.

Caution: All glazed ceramic tile is not equal. In fact, it is best to assume that it's all different. Things to look for include cleanability and slip resistance. Some tiles are hard to keep looking good. Ask for samples to experiment with; even better, ask to see a floor of the exact tile, and check it out. Solid colors, of course, show more abuse than colors with variation.

Try to avoid tiles that become slippery when wet. (Avoid floors entirely that are slippery when dry. Certain waxed floors such as wood, tile, and concrete fall into that category.) Ask about the tiles' slip resistance, and then check sample tiles — wet and dry.

In my experience, certain glazed ceramic tiles make the easiest to maintain floor available. Vacuuming plus periodic wet mopping generally does the job.

Non-Glazed Tile

This tile comes in many shapes, colors, and densities, from irregular handmade to the precisely manufactured "quarry" type. Sealing is required to improve cleanability. Again, get samples and check with suppliers and users for cleaning, sealing, finish, and slip resistance.

Resilient Flooring

Resilient flooring, commonly used in kitchen, bath, utility, and work/hobby areas, is the least expensive applied finish.

The economical choice is the 12″ square tile. For *easier maintenance*, however, sheet vinyl is the way to go.

Sheet vinyl, an excellent basic material, comes in rolls, providing a seamless floor in most kitchen, bath, and utility areas. The coved base (turning the flooring up the wall) simplifies cleaning at the junction of floor and wall.

Most sheet vinyl needs light waxing periodically. Patterns and colors come and go in flooring products, so save leftover material for future replacement pieces.

PETS

A truly low maintenance, easy-to-clean house probably has no pets. Yet, most of us like them, so how to minimize the mess?

One woman said, "I would like a carpet that animal hair doesn't stick to like glue."

If you have this problem with an inside pet, three options come to mind: (1) change the carpet; (2) change the pet; (3) keep the pet off the carpet. If it's a cat, options (1) and (2) apply. If it's a dog, all three options are viable (dogs can be trained to stay out of certain areas).

Cleaning caused by pets relates to your personal preference, such as:

1. Selection of the pet. A lot of control can be exercised here (although I never heard of any bird that didn't make a mess).
2. Inside or outside pet. One or the other is easiest. Both in and out is the dirtiest.
3. Pets access within the house. Pet owners create many of their own cleaning problems. For instance, some owners: (a) allow pets access in and out of the house at will; (b) allow pets full access to the entire house; and (c) allow pets on all furniture.

If you fit the above description, your house cleaning is in a constant state of beginning.

This pet is trained to stop at the edge of the tile. Cleaning becomes easier when pet access within the home is limited.

Interaction is easy for the cook in this kitchen.
Photos by Susan Riley.

Photo by Susan Riley.

Photo by Dave Davis.

Photo by Dave Davis.

A kitchen opening to the dining area is convenient and promotes interaction.

Built-in units keep cleaning to a minimum.

Photo by Mark Boisclair.

A multi-function entertainment center. Photo by Mark Boisclair.

Open planning creates options for multiple function living spaces.

Photo by Dave Davis.

Lighting plays an important role in your enjoyment of living space.

Private spaces, indoors and out.

A well-designed bathroom can offer the perfect space to unwind and recharge.

Photo by Susan Riley.

CENTRAL VACUUM

A built-in central vacuum is a clean, quiet la-bor-saving feature. It's another way to take time and energy out of housework.

Advantages are evident even in an average-sized, one-level house. With a two-story or multi-level house, its value is greater. To quote an Arizona woman, "We live in a tri-level house. Have you ever tried to vacuum stairs dragging a tank behind you?" Another woman said, "My condo has three floors and I wish I had a dustbuster on each floor." Those problems are solved with a central vacuum.

Installation

The visible hardware of a central vacuum in-cludes canister and motor, a long hose with wand, and brush attachments. Interior wall inlets are stra-tegically located and receive one end of the suction hose. Typically, as the hose is plugged in, a relay starts the motor.

Canister and motor (often called the power unit): This unit is located outside your living area, typically in a garage or utility room. Anything sucked into the system ends up in the remote can-ister. Little, if any, dust escapes back into the room

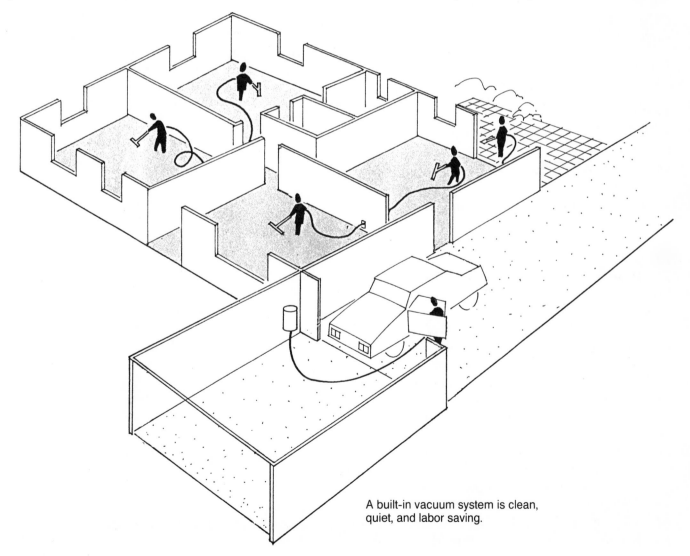

A built-in vacuum system is clean, quiet, and labor saving.

— making a central system quite clean. The remote motor location makes it relatively quiet.

Plastic pipe connects the remote power unit to interior wall inlets. The pipe can be installed in walls, under floors, in ceiling or attic space, or even outside in certain climates. Existing house retro-fit is often possible. Installation in new construction is less expensive.

Check it Out

Like everything, some systems are better than others. Ask the dealer for names of customers to check with. Don't shortchange the motor size. If undersized, it may not do a good job or last long.

Benefits mentioned by users are:

Dust control. Important to allergy-prone people.

Lightweight and convenient.

With the long hose, above-floor surfaces are easy to clean.

Quieter. There's some noise, but not like a portable vacuum.

Less wear and tear on furniture and wall base.

HEATING AND COOLING

Heating systems that force air into rooms will obviously move dust around. However, with a good filter system, it's primarily dust already in the room.

The filtering system with *forced air* is critical. Use good filters and keep them clean.

Radiant heating is a cleaner way to heat. It makes sense in cold climates. But in warm climates, radiant heating can be an expensive luxury. Here is why: When air conditioning is needed, it's sensible to use the same forced-air duct system for both cooling and heating. In that situation, forced air heating is the logical, economical choice.

Air conditioning removes particles from the air by filtering the return air portion of the system. Normally, it's the same filter location for both air conditioning and forced air heating. The same rule

applies — keep the filters clean!

Another cooling system, used in dry climates, is evaporative cooling — basically, air drawn through water-saturated material, blown through ductwork into the house.

Drawbacks to evaporative cooling include: (1) the moisture introduced into your home and, (2) the lack of a good filtering system. Its advantage is the relatively low cost of operation.

FIREPLACE AND SMOKE

Fireplaces create added cleaning and can be a problem for allergy-prone people. They also increase the heat loss from interior spaces. But the charm and good cheer added to a room ensures their place in American homes (certainly in ours).

Several things can be done to reduce the cleaning required. (1) A well-designed and built fireplace

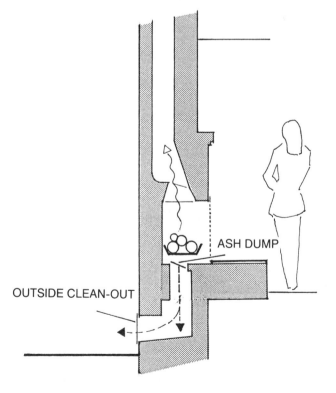

ASH DUMP

OUTSIDE CLEAN-OUT

A fireplace so constructed is easy to maintain.

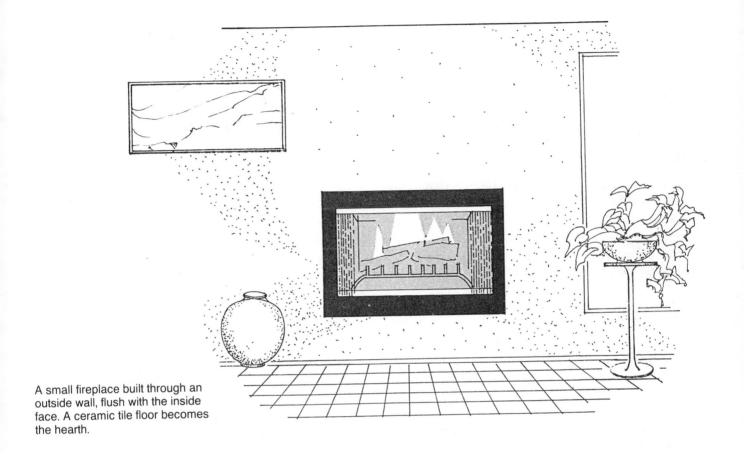

A small fireplace built through an outside wall, flush with the inside face. A ceramic tile floor becomes the hearth.

is a must for clean burning. (2) Have it cleaned regularly from hearth to top of flue. (3) Certain woods burn cleaner than others; always check. (4) Put the fireplace on an outside wall and have a clean-out drop going to an outside opening.

BATHROOMS

The bath has evolved from a place seldom discussed and briefly used to become a temporary refuge in many homes.

For easy cleaning the bath calls for a well-planned area with lots of storage in the right places. When relaxing in a hot tub, exercising, or just pampering yourself, let it happen in an uncluttered, organized atmosphere.

Good planning and selection of materials and fixtures are keys to a bath area that's easy to clean and enjoy.

Planning

The first step is to review your bathroom use habits. Use habits dictate where to locate linen closets, hamper, medicine cabinets, fixtures, towel bars, lighting, wardrobe storage, etc. Good storage for *everything* in and around the vanity area is worth whatever planning time it takes.

When planning baths for children, the same care is needed. This is especially true if one bath is to serve two or more children.

The Bedrooms and Bath chapter reviews planning steps with plans and illustrations.

Materials

Smooth line and smooth materials promote easy care. Don't be led astray by magazine ads showing fussy baths with curtains, drapes, chandeliers, elaborate fixtures, and knick-knacks. Any pleasure derived from that clutter is not worth the pain of extra cleaning. I believe an easily cleaned space with simple fixtures, smooth surfaces, coordinated colors, and good lighting is also better looking.

Colors

Keep maintenance in mind. Solid, dark colors show dust and water spots easily. That applies to all surfaces — counter tops, fixtures, and showers. Carpeting in certain shades of yellow and blue is hard to keep looking good. In walls, off-white to light-medium is a good color range to select from.

Plumbing Fixtures

Easy to maintain plumbing fixtures have smooth lines with few creases and crevices. The same applies to handles and faucets serving the fixtures. A single lever faucet is easier to clean (and quicker to use) than a two-handled model.

Porcelain finished, cast iron tubs and sinks maintain well and have a long life. They are fairly expensive. Plastic/fiberglass units — tubs and showers — may not be as easy to clean, but they cost less.

As always, cost is important and may influence your decisions. The savings accrued *in all areas* — which may include using fiberglass tub or shower — must be weighed against the maintenance factor.

Lighting

The over-decorated bathroom frequently has sparkling chandeliers over the vanity. Not only are they time consuming to clean, but the light quality often is poor. Surface-mounted fixtures require less frequent cleaning.

Better yet, light fixtures recessed in the ceiling seem to need the least maintenance. They can be designed to provide good general room lighting as well as specific task lighting. Either incandescent or fluorescent lamps can be used. Fluorescent lasts longer and the quality of fluorescent lighting is excellent.

There are, however, no hard and fast rules about lighting methods. Factors other than cleanability and easy maintenance come into play. See the chapter on Light for more information.

CLEANING SUPPLIES AND EQUIPMENT

Certain cleaning supplies and equipment (i.e., for baths and kitchens) should be stored in the area to be cleaned. This is especially important in larger or multi-level homes.

"A MAID"

Question: "What would make housecleaning easier?" Answer from many women: "A maid". And from a Pennsylvania woman: "Hiring a maid or not working full-time with three children or a husband who shared equally in housecleaning chores!!"

That woman obviously had some things on her mind. Reading it, I can't help but think back a few years — about my own working wife and our three small children. Some women do amazing things!

Housecleaning services have replaced the "maid" in American homes. There are a lot of them, and quality varies. Almost any arrangement can be worked out — once a week, biweekly, monthly — or simply any time you need help.

Housecleaning help, however, is no reason to forget anti-clutter and easy-to-clean *design*. The longer it takes to clean your home, the more time outsiders will be there and the more you have to pay for the time.

Family cooperation is another housecleaning option; one that is too often missing in a busy woman's life. Certain elements of good building design will encourage cooperation, such as: (1) easy to clean bedroom furnishings and arrangement; (2) open planning to increase interaction; (3) enough storage areas in which to put things. As one woman said, "Storage closets are essential, eliminate a cluttered look, easier to get in mood for cleaning."

In the long run, however, family cooperation doesn't depend on design or planning, but rather on the relationships and responsibilities created within your home.

BUILDING A NEW HOME

Some "experts" say that architects are responsible for house design that creates your cleaning problems. That is baloney, and a cop-out for very real reasons.

Most American homes were not born in an architect's office. However, if you number in the small fraction of those who seek an architect for your next home, *you are in the driver's seat.*

You, the homemaker, *must* dictate your priorities about cleanability! Don't depend on your husband to do it — it probably won't cross his mind. Don't expect the architect to assume that housecleaning is your most important consideration — that is unrealistic.

In pre-design discussions with clients over the last twenty-five years, I can count on one hand the number of women who said housecleaning was a major concern. Priorities usually evolve to a compromise between easy cleaning, aesthetic satisfaction, and keeping the cost down.

Choices between aesthetics and easy cleaning may include a good looking, but harder to maintain floor, wall, or ceiling surface or extra corners and niches that take more cleaning time.

The cost factor may be a choice between an expensive but easier to maintain material and a cheaper but harder to maintain material. The cheaper one often gets the nod.

Make it YOUR business to be involved in such decisions. My problem has never been that women give me too much input regarding their house design. The problem has always been to get you *more*

involved. It's like pulling teeth to get the information needed for your needs, desires, and living habits. *Don't be lazy* in working with a designer. Spend the time — make the effort — give them your priorities!

KNOW YOURSELF

When choosing between easy cleaning, practicality, or excitement and pleasure, you must *know yourself.*

For example, recreational or leisure time items such as a hot tub, sauna, or swimming pool require extra work. Other examples of such choices occur with textured materials for walls or ceiling, or good looking but hard to clean around furniture. Measure the trade-off between the extra pleasure and the extra work.

Of course, many products easy to maintain are also chosen for appearance and pleasure. Look for them. They are out there.

Self Indulgence

Personal pleasure changes the rules. Hobbies that give you pleasure are worth the trouble of cleaning up the mess. We all have our soft spots. With some people it's a pet that creates housecleaning and requires constant care; with others, a collection of artwork to be gladly cleaned around, for the pleasure of their company.

Typically, a few such items are easy to handle, maybe more. But if you build and furnish your home without regard to cleaning and maintenance, you may regret it.

Housework and other "duties" average several hours a day. With a home designed to increase free time, you have raised the quality of your life. When design allows you to interact with others during homemaking, life is more enjoyable.

6
Light

THE RIGHT LIGHT

The right light in a home creates a happy feeling. It's great to hear comments like: "We have a perfect southern exposure for sun in winter." And "Great lighting in kitchen and master bath."

Descriptions like that are, regrettably, the exception. By a margin of four to one, most comments fall the other way. A sampling goes like this: "Poor lighting in kitchen"; "Poor light at sink"; "Poor lighting in all rooms"; "No lights in closets." Second only to the lack of storage, poor lighting is the most common complaint.

For me, a lighting problem is easier to understand than a storage problem. Most of us can visualize the need for storage in various parts of the home. There is no *good* excuse for poor storage. Lighting, however, is another matter.

It's difficult to visualize the amount of light that will enter a space from looking at a drawing. A south wall window provides much more light than the same window in a north wall. Selection of one light fixture over another can mean the difference between a bright or dull space. It's not always easy to know which is the right one. Also, it's hard to imagine how much daylight will enter a space when adding a skylight.

WHY THE FUSS?

Why all the fuss about light? Because it means the difference between cheerful and gloomy, good mood or bad, efficiency or wasted time. Easy to see spaces are easier to clean and maintain. A well-lit kitchen is nicer to work in and even safer.

You should consider two basic types of light — light to make your work easier and your home safer, and aesthetically designed light that adds cheer, warmth, and atmosphere. It is not a case of which type to have. You should have both! And you can, quite easily.

Light for Pleasure

The psychological effect of light is real. Sensations like contentment, anxiety, high spirits, or melancholy are influenced by light and lighting. Our conscious and subconscious are affected.

Light is a great tool to work with. To quote a Utah woman, light levels designed for pleasure mean: "An open kitchen with lots of light — a pleasure to be in." It can also mean good reading lights where you need them, accent lights on paintings and plants, or a restful light in your special place for quiet and reflection. Directional lamps focus your attention, accenting the best features of a space. A series of such lights can make a modest room appear spacious and interesting.

Artificial light is easy to control and creates wonderful mood and effect. Natural daylight, however, can sparkle like nothing else. But it seldom happens by accident. Review each space with your architect or designer. If you are building a new home, study the drawings for the effect of all light sources. If remodeling, estimate where new windows or skylights will create the best effect.

Review Areas and Lighting Needs

Consider the examples listed below. In a typical family or social activity space, the following conditions for lighting might exist:

USE OF SPACE	SUGGESTED LIGHT
a. Traffic circulation	Moderate
b. Conversation area	Moderate, diffused
c. Reading area	Higher level, concentrated or generally brighter
d. TV/video viewing	Low to moderate, indirect
e. Game table	Moderate to high
f. Artwork on walls	Moderate, concentrated
g. Potted plants	Low to moderate, concentrated or general
h. Social function	Moderate, diffused
i. Create mood	Low/moderate/concentrated

Some or all of the above should be found in any average family living space.

Each use area mentioned above may not require its own specific light source. For example, traffic and conversation areas can be served by the lighting needs of an adjacent space. On the other hand, a reading space usually needs its own light source. TV viewing is best when light comes from a source out of direct view.

Design Flexibility — Functional and Artistic

Think about the *use* of lighting in your present or future home. Where is lighting needed and how much? Creating light for traffic, conversation, reading, etc., may involve many lighting options. A partial list is shown below.

1. Indirect lighting
2. Decorative chandeliers
3. Lighting used for displaying artwork
4. Decorative portable lamps
5. Lighting used to accent plantings
6. Pendant fixtures
7. Wall wash, uplighting, downlighting
8. Track lighting
9. Low voltage (12 V.DC) lighting

Good lighting can make a plain room come alive, a cold room warm, or a small room appear larger than it really is. Remember, though, it goes both ways! A room that is exciting by daylight can be dismal at night with bad lighting.

Well designed lighting can direct attention to virtually any part of a room, focusing on a favorite object, painting, or plant. Accenting these points of interest can be subtle or dramatic, depending on the type of fixtures used and the intensity of the lamps.

LOW VOLTAGE LIGHTING

Low voltage lighting, which normally operates at twelve volts, is an application to keep in mind. Its unique features, some of which are noted here, might apply to your needs.

ADVANTAGES:
1. Minimum space requirements.
2. Good effect provided by low intensity.
3. Easy adaptation to most existing structures.
4. Safer for interior and exterior use.

DISADVANTAGES:
1. Selection of fixtures is relatively limited.
2. Switches don't match with regular house voltage switches.
3. Dimming requires special low voltage dimmer controls.
4. Transformers are required to change normal house voltage to low voltage.

5. Replacement lamp cost can be higher and they are not always available in a typical neighborhood store.

Low voltage lamps have a short filament which allows precise control of the light beam. They are especially useful for accent lighting on art objects.

The wiring usually is simple, small, and has less restrictive building code requirements. Therefore, low voltage lighting often is used in do-it-yourself remodeling.

Many bulbs are quite small and can be used with small fixtures for inconspicuous interior application.

Interior fixtures are available in various forms, such as recessed downlights, surface mounted, adjustable, and high intensity pin spots.

Exterior fixtures are available in many forms of accent lighting for trees, shrubs, walkways, steps, patios, buildings, pools, and fountains.

NATURAL PLANNING

Orientation

It sounds so easy, and yet often we don't remember orientation. For instance, windows on the north introduce a colder light and the least light. It's probably not enough for a large space. A living area on the east side will have good morning light, but may be dull in the afternoon when you are likely to be there. Conversely, a breakfast area, which should be bright and cheery in the morning, won't be if it is open only to the west.

Climate

Too little natural light can be harder to correct than too much. Breaking out walls for new openings is expensive and will affect the appearance of your home. On the other hand, some climates are not forgiving to large areas of glass (i.e., north glass in cold climates and south glass in hot climates). There is no need to sacrifice interior comfort for light effect. You can achieve both.

When locating glass, remember that climate, orientation, landscaping, and total glass quantity are factors that influence amounts of heat, cold, and light entering a space.

Effects of Good Artificial Light

Lighting is good when it does the right thing for the space *and* the people in it. It may be balanced light or accent light. It can be designed to enhance the entire space, a single function, or both. To achieve both requires lighting flexibility. Let's look at three methods:

1. Dimmer switches allow you to adjust light levels and atmosphere instantly.
2. Abundant light fixtures, separately switched.
3. Double-switch fluorescent ceilings with some tubes on one switch and the rest on another.

A combination of ample switching (don't put all the lights in a space on one switch), the use of dimmers, and good fixture selection usually will do a nice job.

CLOSETS

There is no excuse for not having good lighting in closets, yet many are *not lighted at all!* Beyond the need to merely find things, you need good light to coordinate clothes, and certainly to clean the space. Such an obvious need deserves no further discussion. One caution — building safety codes do control the location of fixtures in closets. Consult a licensed electrician for the regulation in your area.

SKYLIGHTS

Windows in the roof tell you what the sky is doing — where the sun is, or if rain is coming. You can have nature both ways with skylights. With sunshine, it cheers as it floods the space. Or, hearing the rain beat down, watching it break on the

Dimmer switches allow you to adjust light levels and atmosphere.

DOWNLIGHT

ADJUSTABLE WALL WASHER
WITH BAFFLE AND REFLECTOR

HIGH INTENSITY PIN-HOLE
SPOT (LOW VOLTAGE)

ADJUSTABLE KEYHOLE
ACCENT (LOW VOLTAGE)

Various forms of recessed incandescent lighting which require little cleaning.

ADJUSTABLE EYEBALL

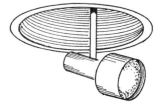

RETRACTABLE ACCENT

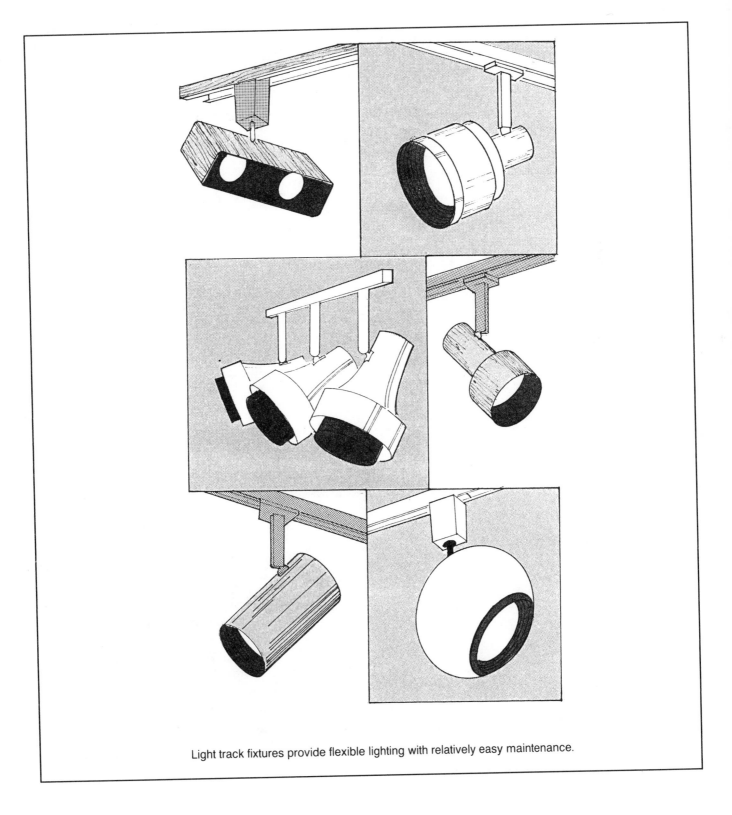

Light track fixtures provide flexible lighting with relatively easy maintenance.

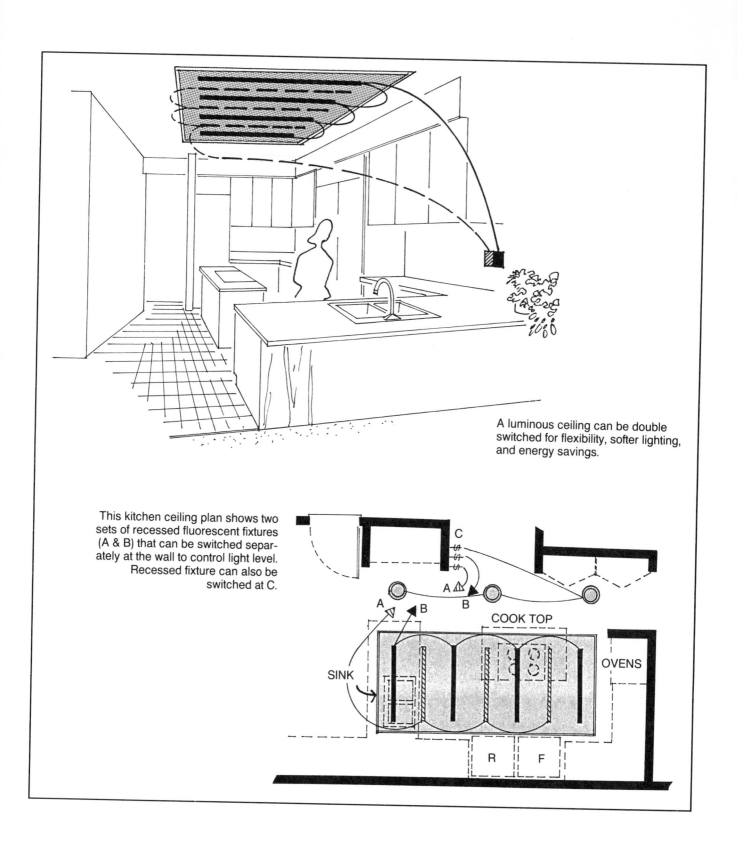

A luminous ceiling can be double switched for flexibility, softer lighting, and energy savings.

This kitchen ceiling plan shows two sets of recessed fluorescent fixtures (A & B) that can be switched separately at the wall to control light level. Recessed fixture can also be switched at C.

COOK TOP

OVENS

SINK

R   F

skylight under a dark sky lets you feel close to nature — and stay dry doing it.

While adding to the enjoyment of a space, skylights improve function. Typical areas for that are: bathroom, kitchen, and work spaces. In areas without windows, such as hallway and utility room, small skylights may provide enough light for daytime use.

Avoid Heat Gain

In hot climates, unprotected skylights can bring high heat inside so that proper location of the openings is important. With a sloping roof, you have greater control of light *and* heat gain. Illustrations here show how it's done.

Even though the light comes to you out of your ceiling, remember that the skylight is actually installed on the roof. With a sloping roof and a flat ceiling, a shaft is built to channel light from roof to ceiling. Note the illustration.

The opposite to heat gain can happen in cold climates with a protected skylight. An adjacent higher wall or a canopy tree shading the sun can greatly reduce the light and heat entering a space. This can be a problem in winter when you want the sun's warming rays through the day.

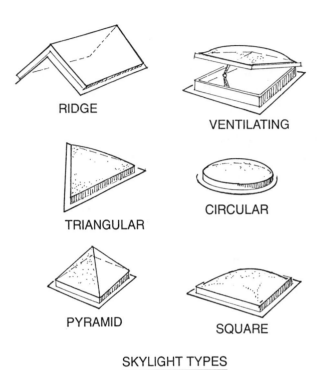

RIDGE

VENTILATING

TRIANGULAR

CIRCULAR

PYRAMID

SQUARE

SKYLIGHT TYPES

SUN LIGHT

CLERESTORY ROOF

HOUSE ROOF

CEILING

This skylight is designed to add natural light and reduce heat gain.

Skylights in Remodeling

Skylights are a useful remodeling tool. The same design factors apply as with windows — basic climate, orientation, and landscaping. Although adding skylights is one of the easiest of improvements to accomplish, many homeowners consistently hesitate to do it! Maybe it's the psychological reluctance to penetrate the roof. Here is a comment from a woman in northern California: "I love the light given by our one skylight and would gladly make our roof look like a piece of Swiss cheese to install more — I can think of five more locations."

I don't go for the "Swiss cheese" look, but there must be some good way to add a few more skylights in that house. It's a matter of doing it!

CREATING A SUNSPACE

A sunspace can be: (1) designed into your new home; (2) a new add-on; or (3) a renovation of existing space. It can bring great joy, frustration, or some of both. It's a matter of planning and your use of the space.

Much of it, of course, depends upon where you live, landscaping, the view, etc. Whether glass walls, a skylighted roof, or both, it usually does mean some form of roof lights for full impact of natural daylight and clear, starlit nights.

Good planning is needed. Professional consultation is advised. Include in your thinking: orientation, sun screening, day and night temperature control, and interior materials exposed to sun rays.

Your sunspace can be both exciting and comfortable. Usually, it's not a typical living space, but one that you will gravitate to for relaxing, reading, socializing — and the pure enjoyment of being there.

With a sloping roof, locate skylights on the north side if you wish to reduce inside heat gain.

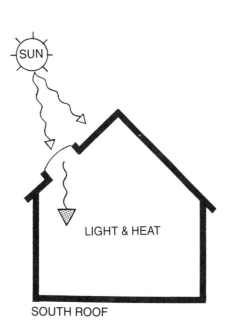

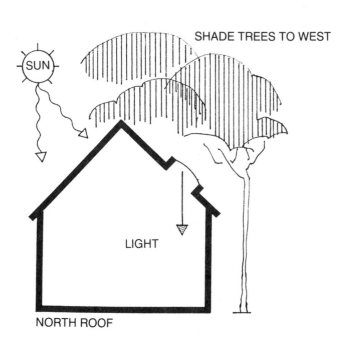

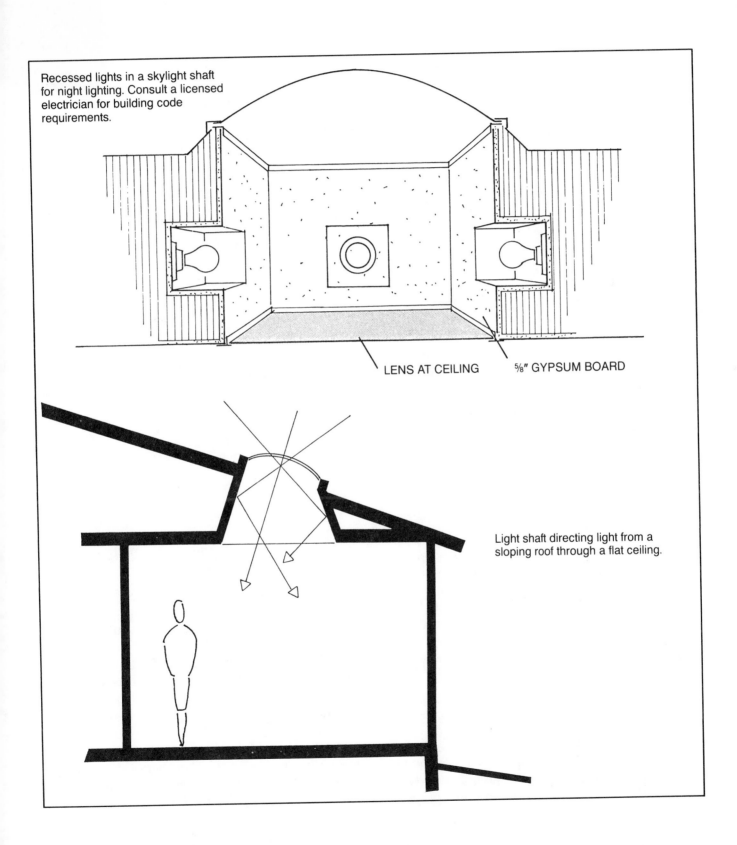

Recessed lights in a skylight shaft for night lighting. Consult a licensed electrician for building code requirements.

LENS AT CEILING   ⅝″ GYPSUM BOARD

Light shaft directing light from a sloping roof through a flat ceiling.

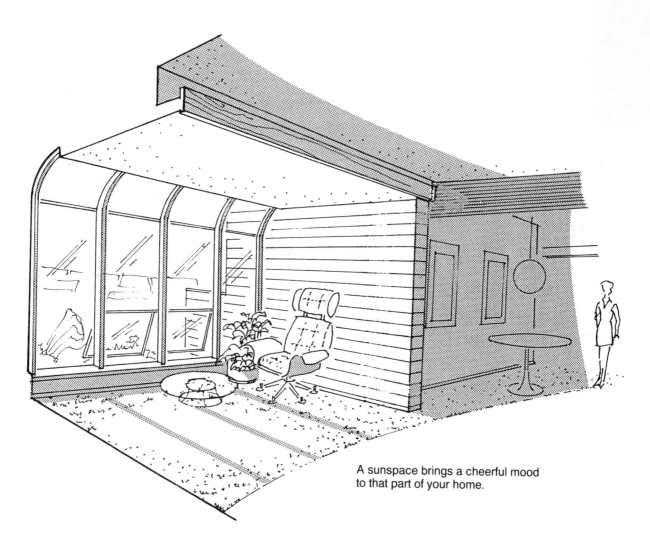

A sunspace brings a cheerful mood
to that part of your home.

LIGHT AND SPACE

When planning a new house, remember the benefits of a bright, cheerful kitchen space. If you are remodeling, it's possible to transform a dull, confined kitchen to a bright, spacious work place.

A small kitchen, shut off from the rest of the house, can be *opened up* and *cheered up* without great expense or adding on. Here are a few ideas that can be used with new construction *or* renovation.

Kitchen Greenhouse

Most of you will have a kitchen window on an outside wall. Consider using a greenhouse type window. They are a manufactured product project-ing out a foot or so, with glass top and sides as well as the window face. Planters in the bottom are usually optional (see illustration).

Borrowed Light

If remodeling, you may have a dining room adjacent to your kitchen and possibly a living space opposite another wall. Decide which walls, or portions of walls, can be removed — opening the kitchen to other spaces. Also, long pass-through counters are often created with no loss of storage or function.

Advantages here are several. Borrowed light from other rooms is one. Another is the feeling of space. A third is the social advantage of interaction with others while working in the kitchen.

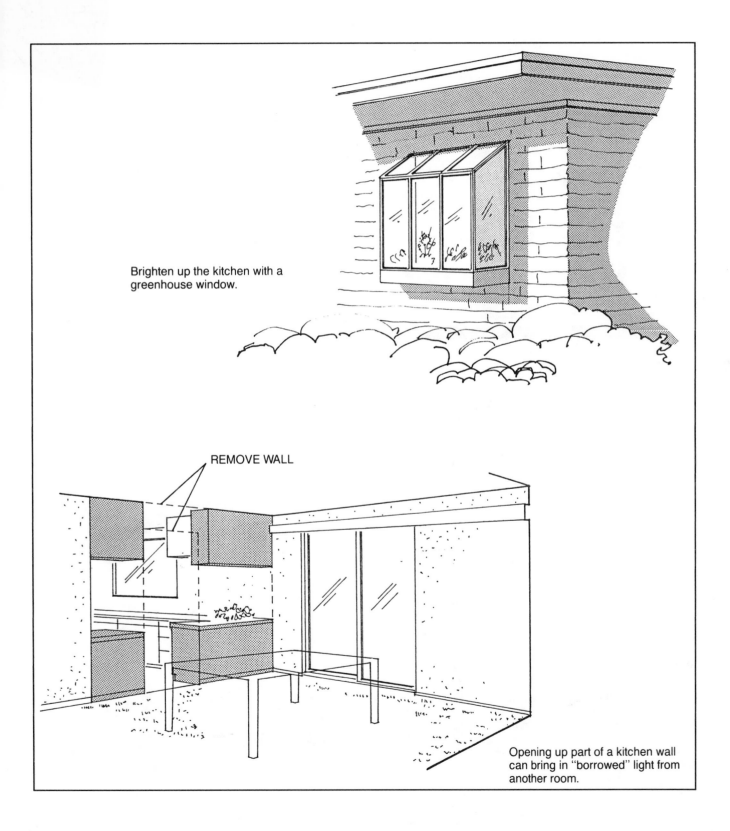

Brighten up the kitchen with a greenhouse window.

REMOVE WALL

Opening up part of a kitchen wall can bring in "borrowed" light from another room.

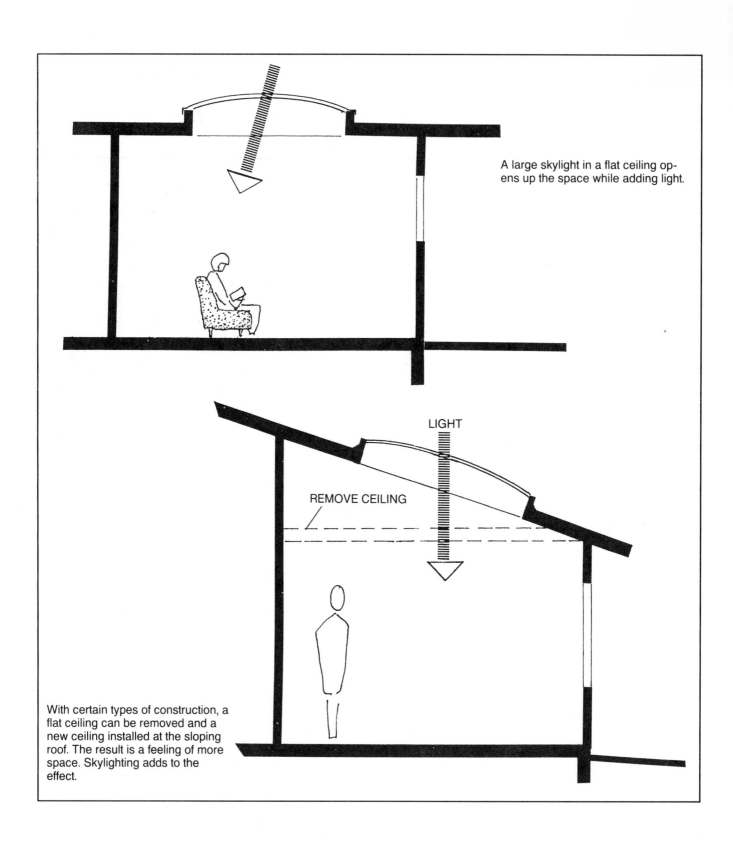

A large skylight in a flat ceiling opens up the space while adding light.

LIGHT

REMOVE CEILING

With certain types of construction, a flat ceiling can be removed and a new ceiling installed at the sloping roof. The result is a feeling of more space. Skylighting adds to the effect.

This high glass provides light with privacy and accents the cedar ceiling.

Open the Top

Don't ignore the space above. Skylights are an obvious option to increase light and a feeling of space. Another is to remove the ceiling and push it up to the roof line. A combination of the higher ceiling and new skylights can create a luxurious feeling in a small space (see illustrations).

STAINED GLASS

We know many effects can be created with stained glass. The trick is to plan what effect you want and where — wall, ceiling, doors, etc. How much impact should it make? Usually try to complement the space rather than dominate (unless the space has nothing else going for it). Stained glass in a large skylight can be a dominant feature, both at the ceiling and because of the reflected, colored light it brings to a space. A more subtle (and economical) approach places it in a niche, a door panel, or within an area of windows.

A small amount of stained glass used to good effect in a door panel.

A narrow stained glass window
brings a nice light to the stair
landing.

A stained glass divider in a home
office-computer setup.

A stained glass chandelier provides
extra pleasure at dining table.

Stained glass adds another dimension to a skylight.

Effect with Economy

Stained glass doesn't have to be a luxury. Small quantities, if well designed, can be very effective. Designed and installed by a craftsperson, it's usually done at a per square foot cost.

The secret to success is the *design itself*, and where it is placed in your home. Where cost is a major concern, don't opt for the large piece, done in cheap glass, by a mediocre designer. Get a small piece for the same cost, but with excellent design and good quality glass.

EXTERIOR LIGHTING

At night, the visual effect of exterior lighting is the introduction to your home. To make it the best introduction, planning is a needed.

Outside lighting of most homes generally relates to function and usually is not planned for aesthetic effect. That's too bad because, for about the same amount of money, fine aesthetic effects can be produced. Various lamps, from bright floods to soft downlights, can create patterns and feelings from subtle to brilliant. The choice is yours.

If building a new home, first design the lighting on paper. To improve your existing home experiments (trial and error) may be needed to get the best result.

Usually, no changes in exterior building or landscaping design are required. It's a matter of adding thoughtful lighting. Ideas for a new or existing home might include:

1. Low lighting of walkways and planter areas, with lamps below the line of sight.
2. Uplighting of high shrubs or trees.
3. Lighting of landscaping from above.
4. Low voltage pond or fountain lights.
5. Light washing on interesting wall surfaces.
6. Backlighting for silhouette effect.
7. Creating a design with the lights themselves.

The Interior Impact

Well done outside lighting can visually improve the enjoyment of inside space. To look out at a well-lighted scene in a courtyard, entrance, or landscaped area is another positive effect.

Many times a nice scene is out there in the dark, just waiting to be lighted. On the other hand, an early benefit of planning outside lighting might be the discovery that there is nothing interesting to look at. Not to worry — that is what pre-planning is for.

Creating something of interest to focus on can be done with landscaping, water, art objects, etc. (The daylight effect is improved at the same time, of course.) Also lights can play on interesting portions of the building.

Security and Safety

Basic security and utility lighting permits safe access, circulation, or congregation. It's something that varies with every home and every homeowner. Steps, ramps, parking, and driveway access are among areas that need to be lighted.

Be careful not to limit your design thoughts only to utility. Again, this is an opportunity to visually add to the immediate environment. Plan the lighting to enhance the landscaping or building surface affected.

Master Switching

For the major indoor and outdoor security lighting, you can provide switching in more than one part of the house. Master switching can be conveniently placed in the master bedroom, with alternate switching located near an exterior door, closer to the light source.

LIGHT AND POWER

A woman in California said, "I have to walk into the dark room to the other side to turn on a lamp." Though it happens often, that is a needless complaint because it's so easy to avoid.

Pay attention to where switches are located *when you are in the planning stage.* Why bother, you say — the electrician will take care of that. Not always.

The electrician knows how to give you a safe electrical system, meeting the building codes. He doesn't know how you plan to use the house, and isn't required to provide total convenience. It's like the rest of your home — get involved and things will work out better.

Convenient lighting happens with fixture placement and switch placement. If two doors enter a room from opposite sides, put a switch at both doors. There is nothing wrong with having two, or even three, switches for the same light.

Another way to avoid groping in the dark for a switch is to navigate with borrowed light from another space. Light reflecting from an adjacent space is more likely to occur with open planning.

A clear example of that is when interior partitions are removed in remodeling. All of a sudden everything seems brighter. Remember also, when renovating, adding a few switches (or light fixtures) normally is not a great expense. And the expense seems even less if an irritation is removed.

In a new home, adding a few extra switches is a negligible expense in relation to the whole.

We hear when so-called "smart" houses are built, lights will go on when you walk into a room. They will stay on while you are in the room, automatically turning off when you leave. It's all available now, but the technology is still expensive. Until it's affordable, we will have to switch them on and off. I prefer that, anyway. In my own environment I enjoy the ability to control the light intensity and quality that affect the atmosphere and function within a space.

I do see, however, real value in "smart" lighting for the purpose of safety and security. Lights that are turned on by switch devices sensitive to movement and sound may indeed contribute to our well being.

Power Outlets

Another California woman, commenting about her home, said: "Not enough electrical outlets . . . I end up with extension cords everywhere."

Yes, I would bet the extension cord business is very good, and has been for some time.

"Poor placement of electrical outlets" happens for the same reason as poor switch location. House builders are required to locate electrical outlets only to minimum building code standards. That means so many feet apart and has nothing to do with your furniture arrangement. So, again, get involved. Arrangement of furnishings, power outlets, *and* switching is relative to your use of the space.

Whether looking at an empty house or a house plan on paper, lay out a probable furniture arrangement. Then, estimate the number of items to be "plugged in." Such items include lamps, TV, stereo, tape player, radio, computers, miscellaneous accessories, games, etc. As closely as possible, estimate where these items will be placed in the room and locate outlets there.

All this may sound too basic to be discussing here. It would be, except that most people don't bother to do it.

Low Maintenance Lighting

Light fixtures usually don't present major cleaning problems, but one or two bad ones can be a constant source of irritation and consume more of your valuable time.

I selected one of those for our own home. It looks nice but requires fifteen minutes to take apart, before careful cleaning even begins.

When selecting fixtures for your home, be concerned about: (1) ceiling fixtures that easily collect bugs; (2) metal fixtures that need to be polished; (3) table and floor lamps that hold the dust and are hard to clean; (4) suspended fixtures or chandeliers that are time consuming to clean; (5) exterior wall brackets and post lights difficult to take apart (dirt and bugs will get inside even if enclosed).

When it makes design sense for your home, select fixtures that are made to be recessed in the ceiling. Cleaning frequency is minimal. The option of fluorescent tubes recessed above a white opal lens flush with the ceiling works well in kitchen and bath. Recessed incandescent, adjustable, and low voltage lights work well in most other areas. Hanging fixtures of simple, smooth design are easier to operate and clean than most table or floor lights.

Good light with low maintenance.

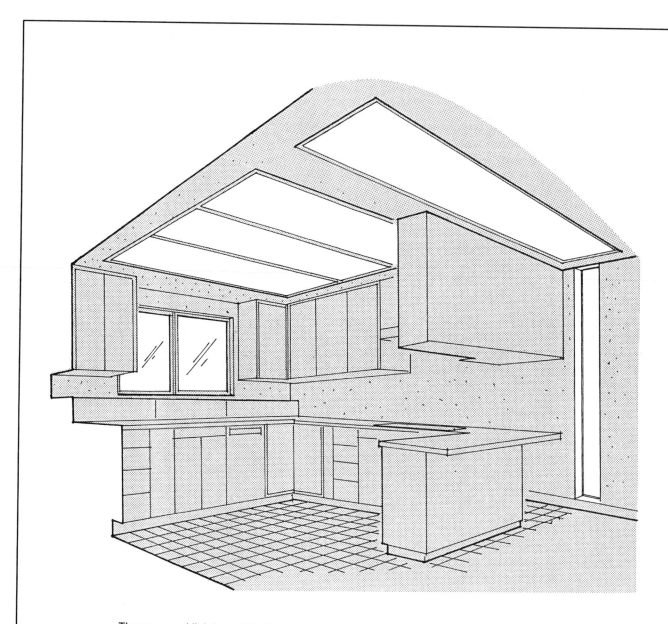

The recessed lighting in this kitchen improves efficiency and is relatively maintenance free.

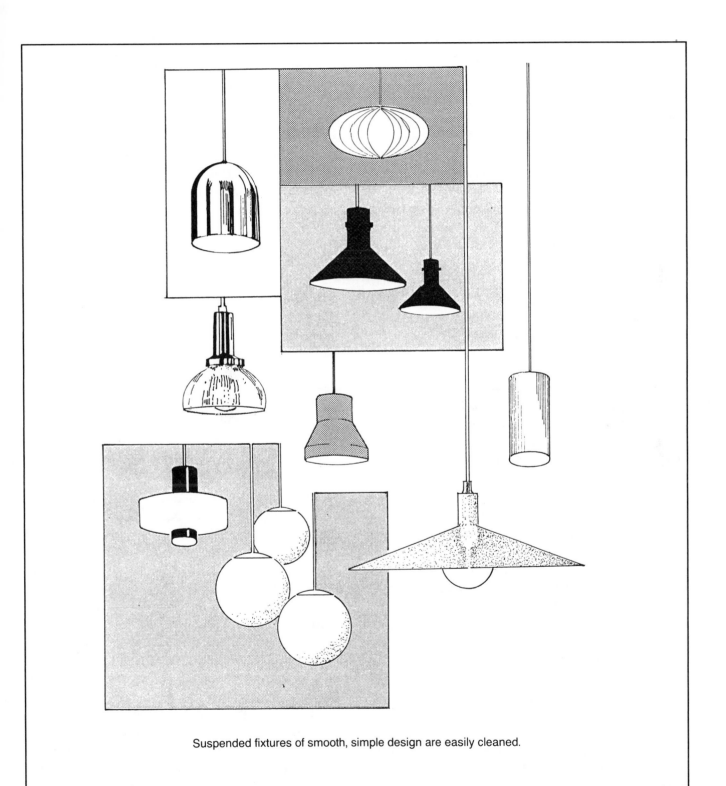

Suspended fixtures of smooth, simple design are easily cleaned.

LIGHT, COLOR, AND TEXTURE

Eight percent of males have defective color vision (commonly called "color blindness"), but only one-half of one percent of females have the problem. Virtually all of you *perceive* colors very well, and how you *see* the colors around you depends upon the light.

Light affects the color of everything — floors, walls, furniture, and people. Different light sources radiate different wave lengths of light. Because of that, each type of lamp (a bulb or tube) will influence the appearance of colored surfaces differently. A woman in Colorado said: "I painted my kitchen yellow so I could pretend it was a fun place to be." That may work for her, but only if the right light source is used.

"Color rendition" describes the effect any particular lamp has on colors. In the early days of fluorescent lamps, colors appeared in ghost-like hues. Incandescent lamps (the common light bulb) influenced colors in other directions. Present-day lamps give us the ability to affect the appearance of an object or space to our choosing. Lamps are available in a color range from sky-blue to orange-red — diverse enough to enhance any decor.

If earth tone reds and oranges are main elements in your color scheme, a warm light source is wise. If blues and mauves are used, cool lamps intensify those colors.

Most lamps used in homes emit color in the intermediate to warm range. (Ironically, natural daylight is a cooler light source.) It's good to remember that even though a "cool" color scheme will be enhanced by a cool light source, the people within the space won't be. That is why lamps in the intermediate range between cool and warm are popular.

The wide range of "colors" from which to choose with fluorescent lamps makes them a good choice for kitchens and bath areas. In these spaces both high efficiency and good color rendition are important.

The Bath

Fluorescent lamps of the intermediate type — between cool and warm — are best for the bath. Consider the makeup area for a working woman. Preparing for the day in a makeup area lighted with warm incandescent lamps is fairly typical. Yet a working woman's day includes exposure to every light source from home, daylight, to work place. For most women, the day is spent in an office — under fluorescent light.

The Home Effect

Lamp type is not the only influence on color and atmosphere in your home. Other factors include the finish used on floors, walls, and ceilings; the texture of furnishings; the intensity of the light itself; and the amount of daylight in the room.

Color scheme of the room decor is an obvious starting place. Trial and error experimentation with lamp types and placement is a good idea, and it's easy to do.

Color Harmony

Background color is critical for creating color compatibility in a space. According to the Illuminating Engineering Society of North America, the most important factor responsible for pleasing color harmony is the lightness contrast between objects within a room and the background walls. The greater the contrast, the greater your chances for good color combinations.

If furnishings and other objects within a room are dark or bright rather than light and neutral, success with those object colors is achieved with off-white to neutral wall colors.

Color and the light source create atmosphere. The psychological effect of atmosphere on your mood is an established fact. It is worth the effort to create the *best* atmosphere. The effort required is not that great and you can have fun doing it.

Lamp Type	Characteristics	Effect on Color
Incandescent	Warm, inviting light	Brightens reds, oranges, yellows; darkens blues and greens
Fluorescent	Wide selection of phosphor colors — select warm to cool lighting atmosphere	Can effectively light any indoor area with a "warm" to "cool" environment as decor or task dictates
	Generally high efficiency for energy consumption	
	Much longer life	

SUMMARY

Start paying attention to lighting in homes — your home and other homes. Note what you like or dislike. Keep in mind quality (interest and atmosphere) as well as quantity (function).

In summary, I have included some lighting reminders for different rooms in your home.

KITCHEN

1. Utility (to see what you are doing).
2. Atmosphere.
3. Consider lighting needs in special places such as: sink and work areas; desk or telephone area; cookbook area; eating area.
4. Wiring for intercom to bedroom and other areas.

DINING

1. Function and atmosphere. Light source can be overhead, wall mounted, and indirect.

FAMILY & LIVING

1. Flexibility, function, economy, and atmosphere.
2. General lighting for ease of circulation and to make spaces appear cheerful, comfortable, and well balanced.
3. Reading areas.
4. Games and recreation.
5. Accent areas (plants, paintings, sculpture, etc.).
6. Power outlets in floor for mid-room lamp fixtures.

ENTRY

1. Inside and outside. Security, access, and atmosphere.

BEDROOMS

1. Master bedroom. Do you want master switching here for areas inside and outside the house/
2. Low wattage night lights.
3. Wiring for intercom.
4. Light fixture in center of ceiling is often not the best location. Alternate locations are:
   a. A light in front of a closet.
   b. Lights on paintings or decorative objects.
   c. Lights at reading chair or night stand with three-way at bed.
   d. Indirect lighting.

7
Furnishings

Unless you live in a furnished apartment, furnishings are something you can directly control.

Furnishings reflect your personality (bright and cheerful, of course!), taste, and lifestyle. Unless your home interior is architecturally unique, the furnishings probably create the strongest of all visual impressions in any one space.

The design, color, texture, and arrangement of furnishings work together with lighting, floors, walls, and ceilings — the architectural space itself — to create the atmosphere. Good atmosphere is harmony of form and color, and the feeling of completeness.

Putting together furnishings is fun — whether on a tight budget or free-spending. In fixing up old furniture or buying new, imagination helps. Also, it helps to have two plans of attack, one for selection and one for arrangement.

It's easy. Let's first look at criteria for selection.

SELECTION

Design

A well-designed piece of furniture is good looking and functional. It looks good standing alone in a space, or fits in with many different surroundings. You don't tire of looking at it.

The best design is not "trendy," nor does it represent a certain period. Trendy design, like "pop art" or "post modern" architecture, represents fads that are usually short lived. They flourish in periods of creative absence and then become tiresome.

Select furniture because it's well designed, well made, and complements your planned arrangement and architectural space.

Quality and Value

Don't compromise with quality. Take your time. You will probably keep your furniture for a long time. Let *value* be a guideline.

Value means getting what you want at a fair price. To some that means furnishing an entire room for the price others might spend for a chair. To another, it's finding that one item you have been looking for — at an affordable price.

If you develop a master plan for furnishings, you won't have to compromise with selection. Acquire the pieces gradually, as you find them and can afford them.

When building a house or remodeling, do a furniture layout along with the house planning. Then you will have time to shop for good values or have built-in pieces made. Special order furniture, if necessary. It's sometimes the only way to get the right color, fabric, wood finish, etc., to complement the whole scheme.

If you special order, do it early in the building or remodeling phase. Delivery time from factories is *slow*.

Upholstered Furniture — Maintenance

Why are some homes easy to clean and others a nightmare? Look at the furniture — type and arrangement — for part of the answer. How can the type of furniture affect housework? Easy. It doesn't take long to separate high and low maintenance furniture.

Upholstered furniture requires care in selection to avoid maintenance pitfalls. Some features leading to high maintenance are:

1. Loosely woven fabric that catches and moves.
2. Solid colors.
3. Tufted backs or seats.
4. Very light colors (depending upon user habits).
5. Easily soiled material — also hard to clean — like real suede.
6. Seating supported on legs, especially short legs.

Easier to maintain upholstered furniture includes the following:

1. Tightly woven fabric.
2. Medium toned colors.
3. Fabric woven in prints or patterns.
4. Smooth surface pieces with attached cushions.
5. Seating built solid to the floor — no hard to reach space underneath.

Hard Surface Furniture — Maintenance

Features that promote high maintenance time in *hard surface furniture* include:

1. Elaborate woodwork — carved, notched, fluted, etc.
2. Wood that marks easily — soft, light, or dark.
3. Glass top tables — considered easy to clean by some, will show every fleck of dust under certain light.
4. Any intricately made piece with lots of separate members, supports, cross bars, etc.
5. Hardware that is attached, protrudes, is figured or ornamented.

Low Maintenance:

1. Wood not easily marred — hard, medium toned.
2. Pieces made with smooth, clean, flat surfaces.
3. Beveled or rounded edges for quick cleaning.
4. Base in solid material flush to the floor.
5. Flush, clean surface hardware, or doors and drawers made to open without hardware.
6. Plastic — not the cheap, easily damaged variety, but well made, strong, molded plastic with rounded edges can be low maintenance furniture. It can also be expensive.

BUILT-IN FURNITURE

Built-in furniture is a way to save space and, sometimes, money. Another advantage is that furniture will be in place when construction is complete. A disadvantage is that the custom and fixed in place arrangement is hard to change and might inhibit resale of the home to certain people.

SOURCES

If you find the right pieces in familiar stores — great! If not, don't give up, there are other sources. Here are a few ideas:

1. Office furnishing stores often stock chairs, sofas, lamps, and other items applicable for home use. Get on their mailing list for sales.
2. Go beyond the larger outlets. Small independent furnishing stores often stock high quality, well designed pieces. Ask to be placed on their mailing list and notified of upcoming sales.
3. Consider ordering from catalogs of fine furniture. A salesperson will often work with you from their library of catalogs and fabrics, or you can work with a designer or architect.
4. If you select an independent consultant, your range of choices might be greater. They should have knowledge of what is available and where to find it. Get specific about their fees and furniture costs, and define your budget.

5. You can have fine furniture hand made, rather than buying ready made. This way you get exactly what is best for the room, and sometimes at a lower price. For best results, first have it designed and drawn on paper. Common items to acquire this way are: bedroom furniture, stereo and TV cabinets, bar units, tables, and most other items made of wood or metal. Seating areas also can be designed and custom made, bid, and built in.

STORAGE WITHIN

Storage within the furniture is discussed throughout this book for several reasons:

1. It's a good way to have things available where they are used.
2. It helps reduce clutter in a home with small spaces and too few closets.
3. It's great for renters who must take whatever storage comes with the place — never enough.

Creating the Space

Whatever the piece of movable furniture, if it goes flush to the floor — without legs — you have a potential storage cavity.

Types of furniture commonly used for storage include: bed, sofa, and tables of all kinds — coffee, end, and side tables.

Built-in furniture offers the most potential for extra storage and can be created to fit the space.

COLOR

When colors in a home contribute to the warm, cheerful, and inviting feeling some homes have, often it's because they were selected as part of an interior master plan. Colors for furnishings, floors, walls, and ceilings, were selected and blended while the space was still empty. Accessories and art objects are obtained to complement or accent the basic scheme.

No, this is not the only way to succeed with a color scheme. And yes, someone good with colors can work with wild abandon and pull off a stunning success.

What I described above is a method for most people to achieve a pleasant scheme of colors. Typically, furniture colors are chosen not for themselves, but for how they combine with all objects within a space. Furnishings *complement* the carpet, light fixtures, accessories, and wall hangings.

Furniture colors will *contrast*, however, with the *walls* of a space. Usually, the lightness contrast between objects within a space and the walls results in a good combination of colors. Lightness contrast does enhance our spatial perception.

ART AND ACCESSORIES

It's a rare home that doesn't display some form of art — paintings, sculptures, prints, etc. Never enough, for most of us!

Invariably, the art object we like is too expensive to buy. However, although it does take some looking, good artwork is obtainable. Listed below are a few typical sources:

1. ART GALLERIES: The obvious choice, and usually thought to be expensive, they often carry work of new artists at a reasonable cost. Also, check out their supply of print and poster art. Get on their mailing list.
2. ART OR CRAFT GUILDS: These groups are found in every town and often are a source of much art work. Outdoor art festivals have become popular and are a rich (and inexpensive) source of original art, especially watercolors.
3. DEPARTMENT STORES: Often overlooked by the serious shopper, some stores carry fair quality prints of good work, at reasonable prices.
4. COLLEGES AND UNIVERSITIES: These are fertile areas for original art at a good price. Watch for exhibits of student or faculty work. There is a constant production of new work, from new people, every year.

5. THE ARTIST: Don't be shy about contacting artists to buy directly. Also, it's a way to get a custom piece of work for that special place in your home.

ARRANGEMENT

Selection is only half the fun. Arrangement of furnishings is the other key to an interesting space.

Keep it simple! A common mistake with furnishings is to do too much. Most homes are over-furnished — to the point of clutter.

Compose furnishings for function, but always aesthetically. Good features, in artistic compositions, are enhanced by the empty space around them. So it is with a good-looking piece of furniture.

Also, a room not over-furnished is a versatile space — good for that occasional multi-use activity.

If Room is Too Small

The following scenario is not uncommon, particularly with multi-purpose spaces.

No matter how many ways you plan the furnishings, there often are two or three things trying the occupy the same space. Several options are open:

1. The obvious — omit some furniture.
2. Find or build in furnishings that are smaller. There is a big difference in overall size of furniture used for the same task — from seating to pianos, pool tables, desks, stereos, and TVs. You can select or build in items to a scale to fit the space.
3. Make the space larger. Door placement and door swing can either increase or decrease the space needed for furniture, traffic, and circulation. Pocket or folding doors may help a space problem. With this in mind, check the door type and arrangement in the design stage.

Planning Ahead

The furniture arrangement for a new home, or a remodeled space, should be part of the basic house design. Don't wait until construction is complete and then shoe-horn in the furnishings. The arrangement goes with the space and should be laid out, on paper, as the room is planned.

Remember the habit trap! Your existing floor plan dictated the arrangement (and often the type) of furniture. In a new or renovated space that should not happen. Decide first how you want to use the space. Then plan the space and furniture layout together to make it happen. In furniture selection and arrangement, think about the following features in your planning:

1. FUNCTION: How will the furniture be used? This relates to size, durability, type of material, comfort, and construction.
2. TRAFFIC: Review the expected traffic flow throughout the rooms. Don't let your furniture arrangement interfere with logical traffic flow! A slight interference may work, but more than that will be a constant irritation.
3. COLOR, TEXTURE, AND FINISH: Color, texture, and finish in furnishings help establish the atmosphere. Colors, warm or cold, lights or darks, etc., affect the mood of a space. Therefore, the selection process should take place when choosing the finishes and colors of the room itself. A side benefit of this method is that you won't make hurried, last minute choices.
4. ACOUSTICS: Floor covering, seating, wall coverings, and ceiling material all act to either increase or dampen the noise level in a space.
5. LIGHTING: Plan your lighting to complement furniture, art objects, and basic room plan. Some lighting might be built in, such as ceiling spots, wall washing, or general illumination. Other lighting will be part of the furniture, such as table and floor lamps or wall-mounted fixtures.

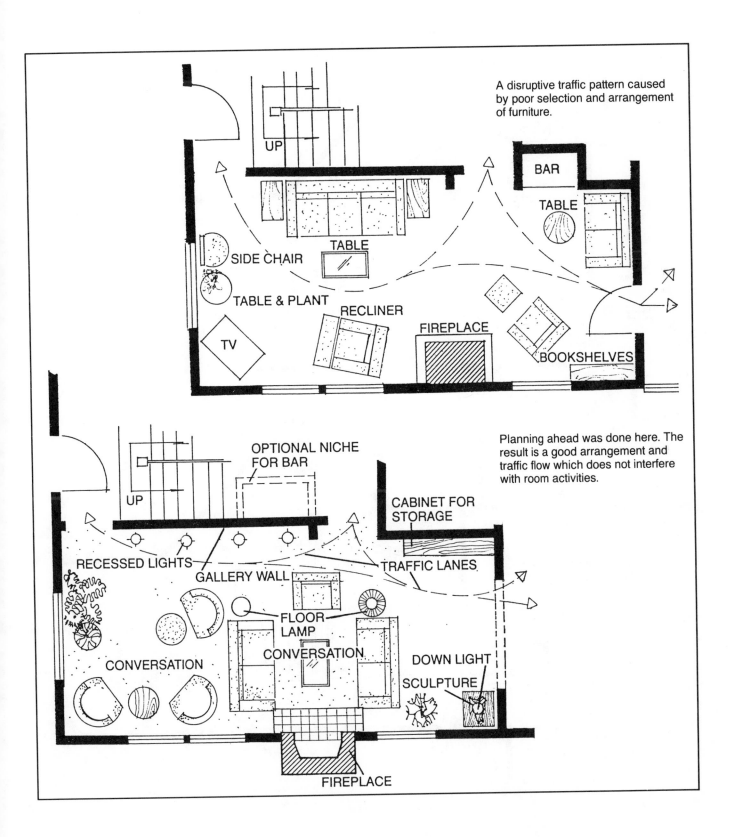

A disruptive traffic pattern caused by poor selection and arrangement of furniture.

UP

BAR

TABLE

SIDE CHAIR

TABLE

TABLE & PLANT

RECLINER

FIREPLACE

TV

BOOKSHELVES

Planning ahead was done here. The result is a good arrangement and traffic flow which does not interfere with room activities.

OPTIONAL NICHE FOR BAR

CABINET FOR STORAGE

UP

RECESSED LIGHTS

GALLERY WALL

TRAFFIC LANES

FLOOR LAMP

CONVERSATION

CONVERSATION

DOWN LIGHT

SCULPTURE

CONVERSATION

FIREPLACE

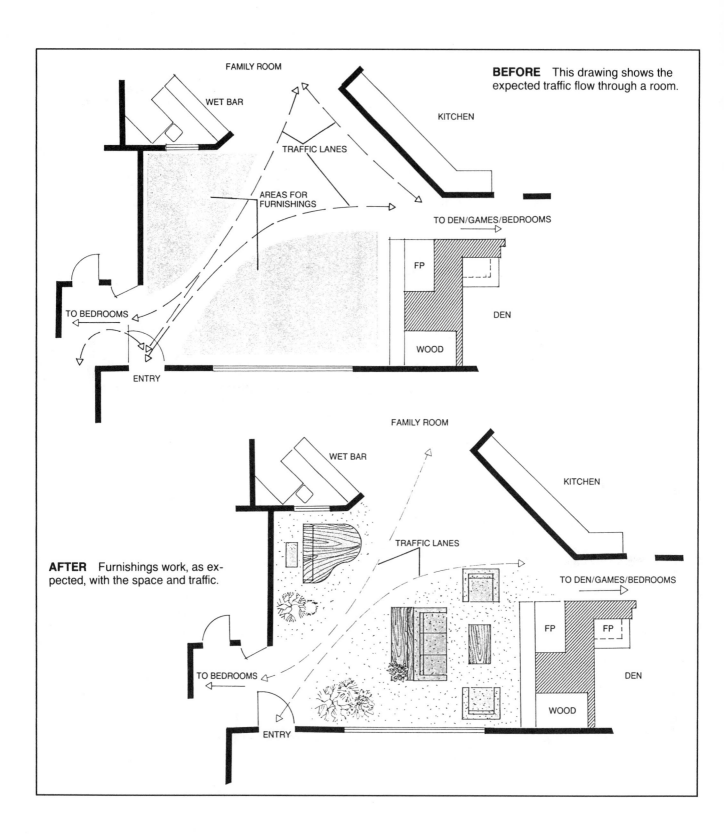

FAMILY ROOM

WET BAR

BEFORE This drawing shows the expected traffic flow through a room.

KITCHEN

TRAFFIC LANES

AREAS FOR FURNISHINGS

TO DEN/GAMES/BEDROOMS

FP

DEN

TO BEDROOMS

WOOD

ENTRY

FAMILY ROOM

WET BAR

KITCHEN

TRAFFIC LANES

AFTER Furnishings work, as expected, with the space and traffic.

TO DEN/GAMES/BEDROOMS

FP   FP

DEN

TO BEDROOMS

WOOD

ENTRY

NOTE: Don't forget that different types of lighting will affect the color of everything you see. It's quite possible that you will select carpet and furniture shown under fluorescent lamps in a store. Paint may be selected from color swatches under different light. Paintings, hangings, etc. might be shown in outdoor space. And yet the space in your home, to contain all of the above, probably will be lighted with incandescent lamps.

The point is, when possible, assemble samples of the various materials and surface treatments you are considering. Then, evaluate them under lighting conditions similar to those which will be present in your home.

Recessed lighting complements the decor while generally lighting the area.

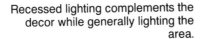

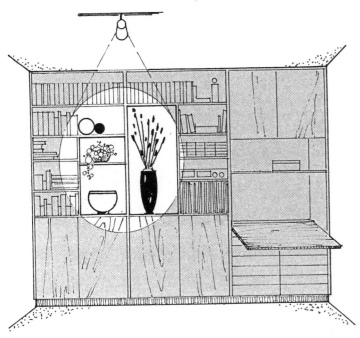

Directional track lighting is used for special effect with furnishings and accessories.

8
There's Always a Way to Increase Storage

Every home has room for more storage. This chapter will help you find it.

Asked what feature of her home gave her the most benefit, an Oregon woman said: "Enough storage in each area for getting at things quickly, where you need and use them."

General storage is anywhere and for everything. Open shelving is one way, but normally we are storing things we don't want seen.

Other chapters include storage tips for specific areas of the home. This will be an overview chapter, looking for storage *potential*, without adding onto the house.

FINDING STORAGE SPACE

The next statement came from a "housebound husband" who handles household duties while his wife works: "I think most homes have adequate storage that is not used because of lack of imagination." I don't *exactly* agree with him, but I do think most homes have the *potential* for adequate storage.

Lack of imagination is one cause. Combine that with inertia, and you've got a common condition. *We all tend to accept what we're given with a house.* Changes, even small ones, come slowly.

A Michigan woman said, "If we had easier storage (closets, etc.), there would be less nagging about keeping rooms tidy." I hope to convince you that there is no excuse not to improve storage and free your home of clutter.

Household clutter ensures wasted time and frazzled nerves. A prime reason for clutter is "not enough storage." Asked what would make housecleaning easier, a Toronto woman said, "More storage, so things could be put away instead of moving them every time I clean."

INCREASE STORAGE WITHIN EXISTING SPACE

Storage space comes in many forms. It is either found or created. There is *always* a way to create extra storage space. Believe that, please, and go looking. With pen and pad in hand, check every room, closet, nook, and cranny. List areas with *potential* for more storage, no matter how slight the potential. You will be surprised how long the list becomes.

Before you make the list, note items that typically are *looking for a place to be stored.* For instance, it's a rare home that doesn't have paper, in all its forms, lying around. From an Arizona

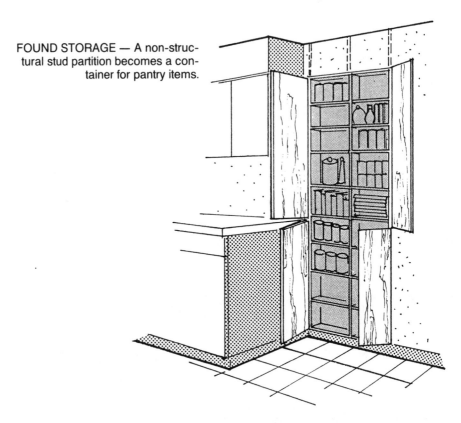

FOUND STORAGE — A non-structural stud partition becomes a container for pantry items.

woman: "There is never enough hidden storage space. There are so many excess papers that are part of life — the problem of finding a place for 'stuff' becomes a way of life." She is right.

In-wall Storage

Non-supporting stud-wall partitions are natural storage containers. An example of "found" storage for small items is the space between the studs. It's very useful if you're in a small home or condo for pantry and small storage items (see illustration).

An example of "created" storage is to increase the depth of a stud wall partition to create storage wall cabinets (see illustration).

Much will fit into a 10" or 12" deep space. For instance: cleaning supplies and equipment, sports equipment, games, paper, tools, books, portable appliances, bar items, seldom used cookware, dishes,

linens, etc. This type of space also can be used as extra wardrobe hanging space with items hung from an extended hang bar (see illustration).

A *"created" storage wall* can be attractive. The entire wall should be designed before building. Select materials and hardware carefully and have finish work done by a craftsman.

NOTE: Several times throughout the book I discuss between-the-stud or in-wall storage. It is important to note here that I do not advocate using a bearing wall for this purpose. Use a non-bearing (non-supporting) wall, and *never* cut through one of the studs. The typical space available between studs in a wall is about 14½". When creating a new storage cavity, it's a good idea to line the space with one-hour rated drywall.

Use care to determine that there are no electrical or plumbing lines within the wall in the area of the proposed storage. If you can't determine if a

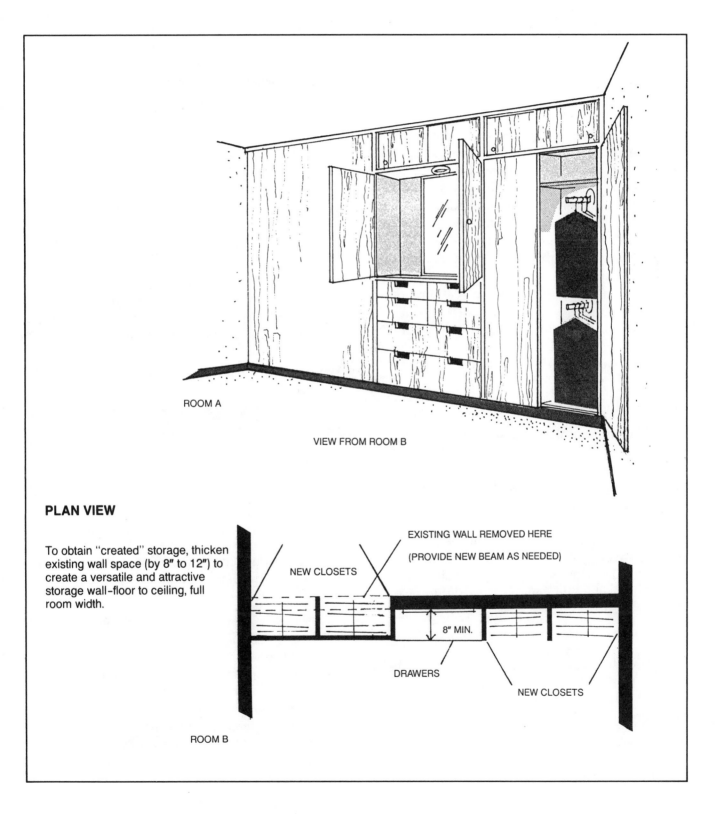

ROOM A

VIEW FROM ROOM B

PLAN VIEW

To obtain "created" storage, thicken existing wall space (by 8″ to 12″) to create a versatile and attractive storage wall–floor to ceiling, full room width.

NEW CLOSETS

EXISTING WALL REMOVED HERE

(PROVIDE NEW BEAM AS NEEDED)

8″ MIN.

DRAWERS

NEW CLOSETS

ROOM B

wall or partition is non-supporting, or contains electrical or plumbing lines, ask for help from an engineer or local building official.

Basement

The basement is a good storage area, but commonly misused. At move-in time, things that have no assigned space are put there. Gradually boxes are added to boxes, corners fill up, walls are covered. Possessions begin creeping out onto the floor. Clutter on a big scale takes over. Before you know it, you can't even remember what is down there.

Organization is the key to good storage anywhere. It's especially important in basements, thus leaving room for functions like recreation, hobby, workshop, etc.

Whether you build shelving, cubicles, hanging racks, etc., or buy them ready made, organize for *maximum storage in the least space.*

Organization Pitfall

There is another benefit to good storage. It makes inventory easy, helping you find things in a hurry. There is a pitfall, too. Good organization gives you more places to store junk — junk being defined as something you should have thrown away instead of storing in the first place.

A way to improve storage habits is to label the contents of every shelf, bin, or box. It's a time saver thereafter. In addition, forcing yourself to label a worn-out, useless item makes it harder to save.

Attic

Attic storage is similar to basement storage. But I can think of two important differences that affect what is stored there — temperature and structure.

1. Temperature: Items that benefit from a cool place are candidates for the basement. An attic is hotter. Depending on your climate, it can be a *lot* hotter. If the space isn't well insulated and cooled, beware of what is stored there. Paper and rubber dry out, photographs can stick together and wood joints loosen.
2. Structure: Attic floors are seldom built to hold storage loads. (When converting attic space to living space, the same precautions should be taken.) So, *have it checked* by a structural engineer or local building official.

Furniture

Many furniture pieces serve double duty and can be used for storage. Examples include:

Tables such as corner, end, occasional, coffee, etc., customized for storage, to keep things where needed. (NOTE: In-furniture storage is especially useful in rental space such as a condo or apartment.)

Window seats make good storage — either a bin or drawers.

Organized under-bed drawer storage.

Sofa seating with storage drawers underneath.

One of the best applications of in-furniture storage is to have furniture designed to fit the space and situation.

Kitchen

These ideas can help maximize storage in your existing kitchen and eating area without adding space to your home.

1. Provide roll-out lower cabinet shelving for access to rear of shelves.
2. Add lazy susan at inside corners.
3. Install adjustable shelving in cabinets. (Check stability and attachment of upper cabinets when increasing storage.)
4. Add 3½" deep cabinets between non-supporting wall studs, at exposed wall areas.
5. Install vertical dividers in left-over skinny vertical space.

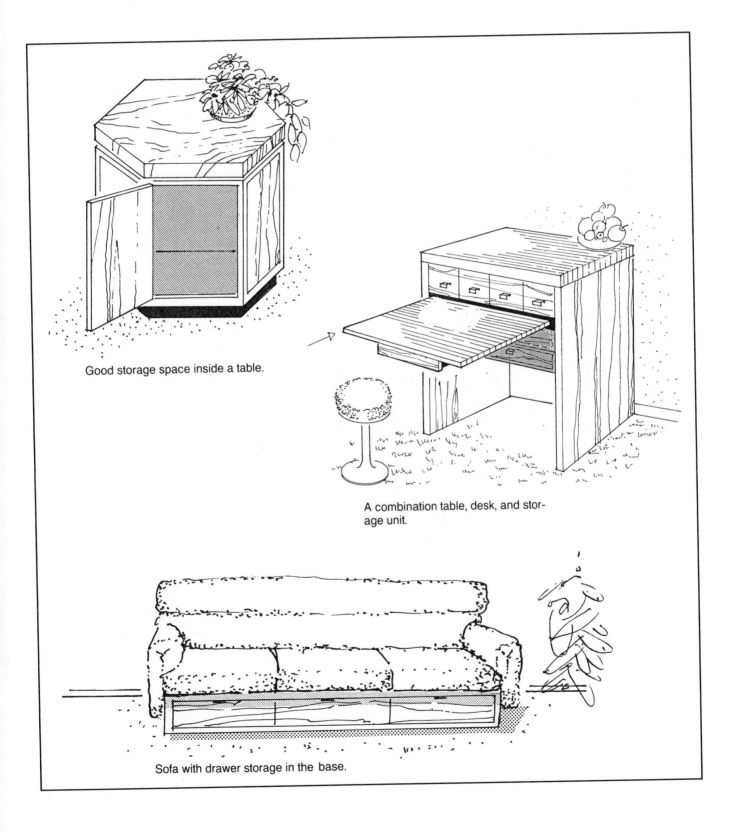

Good storage space inside a table.

A combination table, desk, and storage unit.

Sofa with drawer storage in the base.

6. If you can afford to lose 18″ to 24″ of counter space, add a floor to ceiling full counter-depth storage cabinet, 18″ to 24″ wide. It is effective use of space, and works best at the end of a counter. Use roll-out shelves.

7. If you have a wasted outside corner, add a storage niche or cabinet in this space.

8. In the under-sink cabinet, add side shelves adjacent to plumbing, or add roll-out wire shelving made for this space.

9. Add racks or shallow shelving on the inside face of closet doors.

10. When replacing cabinets, extend upper cabinets to ceiling. The top space, otherwise wasted, is good for seldom used items. (At the same time, provide nearby storage for a sturdy stepladder for access.)

NOTE: The Convenience chapter explores general kitchen design.

With roll-out shelving, the entire shelf, front to back, is used.

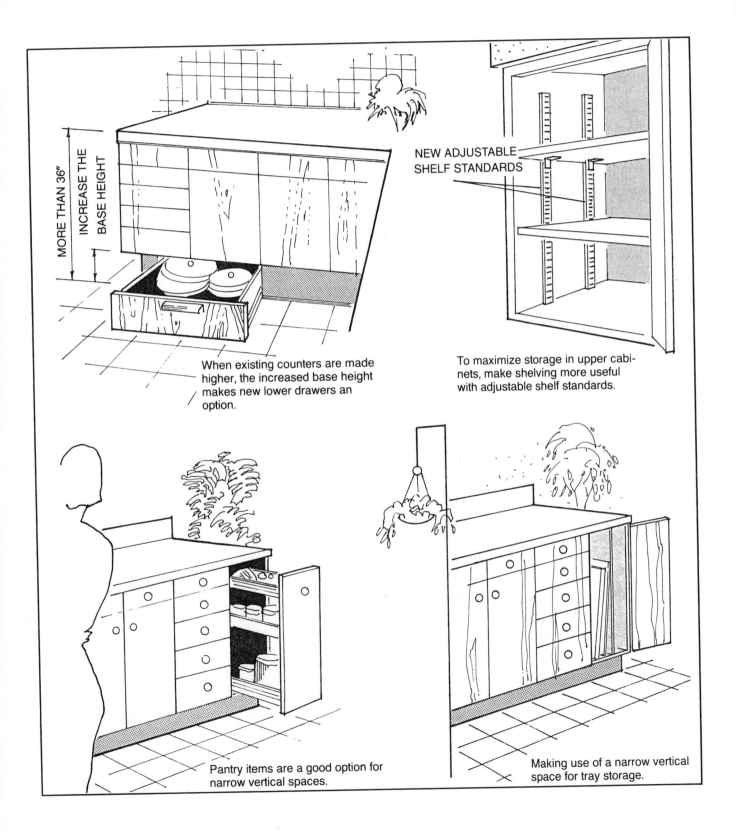

When existing counters are made higher, the increased base height makes new lower drawers an option.

To maximize storage in upper cabinets, make shelving more useful with adjustable shelf standards.

Pantry items are a good option for narrow vertical spaces.

Making use of a narrow vertical space for tray storage.

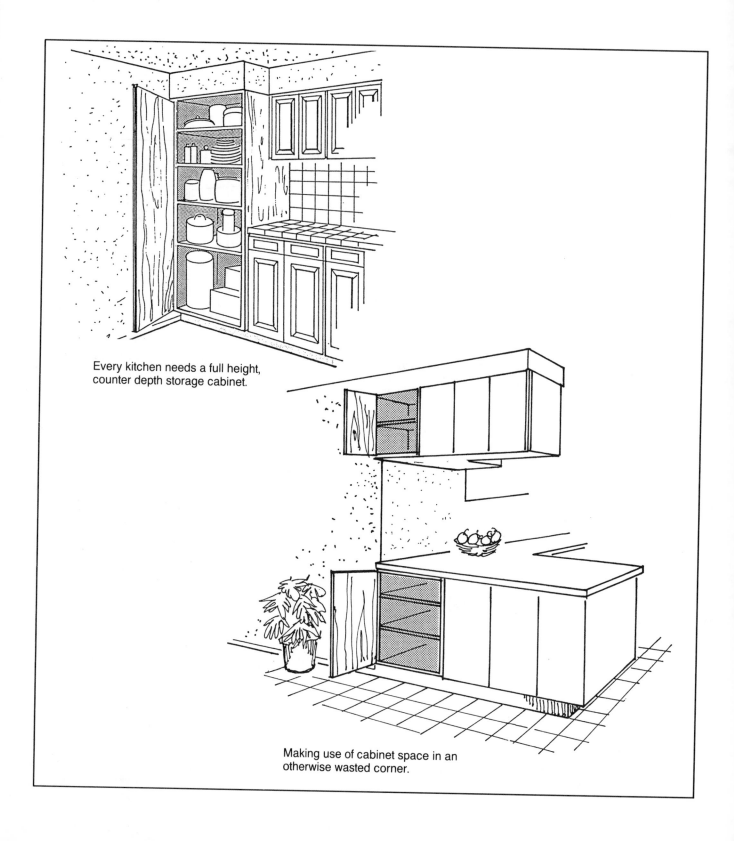

Every kitchen needs a full height,
counter depth storage cabinet.

Making use of cabinet space in an
otherwise wasted corner.

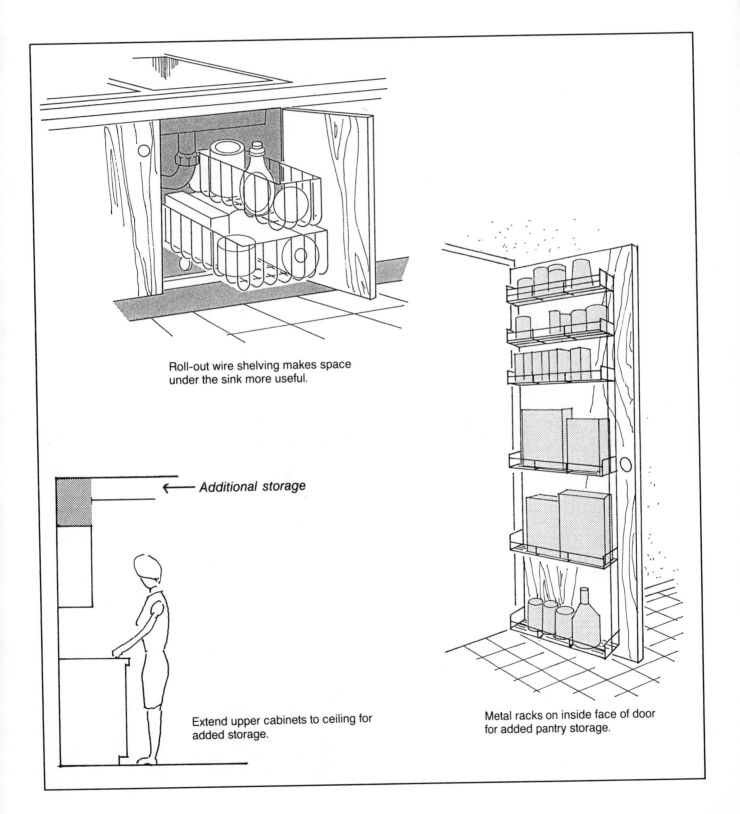

Roll-out wire shelving makes space under the sink more useful.

← *Additional storage*

Extend upper cabinets to ceiling for added storage.

Metal racks on inside face of door for added pantry storage.

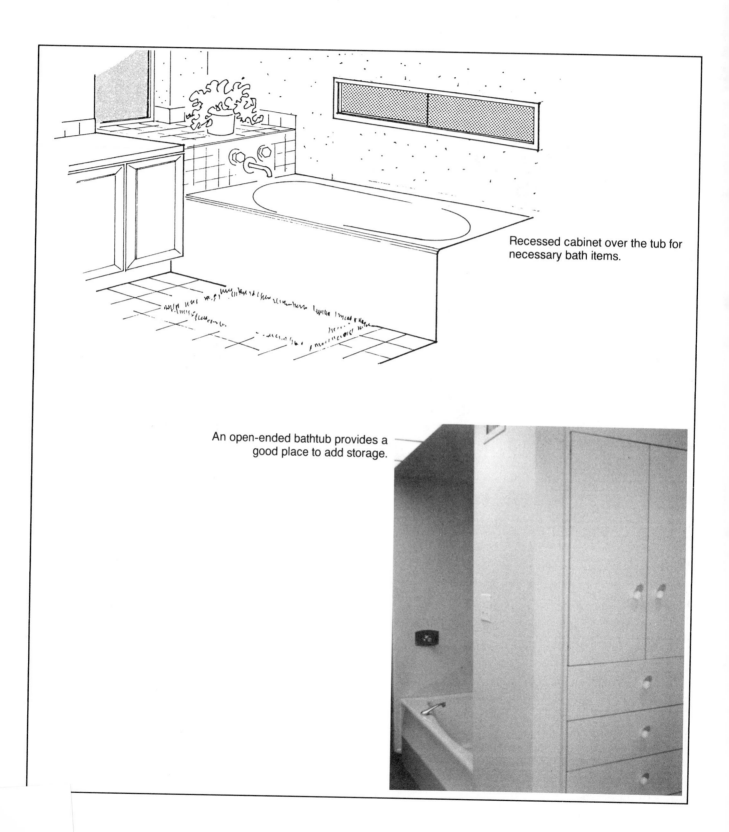

Recessed cabinet over the tub for necessary bath items.

An open-ended bathtub provides a good place to add storage.

Replan Your Closets

Starting the day, putting away laundry, taking inventory of your wardrobe, getting ready for work; all of the above go faster in direct proportion to storage organization.

Have you ever heard the statement, "I can't get another thing in that closet?" *It's probably wrong,* and that goes for any kind of closet.

We have established that there aren't enough closets and what we have are too small. Don't compound the problem with poor use of those we have. Get them organized.

How important is closet planning? Important enough to support an industry called "closetology." If rebuilding closet interiors is a stumbling block, a "closetology" service can do the job. Better still, take the challenge yourself and create order out of chaos. By redesign, you might add enough storage in existing closets to meet your needs.

Check do-it-yourself stores for shelves, racks, hangers, and modules to help consolidate. The plastic-coated wire products make for easy cleaning.

A well-planned closet, however, is wasted effort if it's crammed with unused bulk. Rebuilding closets is a perfect time to eliminate junk.

Take Inventory

Take inventory of your possessions. Analyze their storage worth according to frequency of use — often, seldom, yearly, or not in the last ten years! Decide what you can do without and never miss. Then give it away!

Every Nook and Cranny

After the closets, look for other possibilities. Find corners and niches where cabinets can be installed. In-wall storage, wall cabinets installed over counters, beds, toilets, and tubs can work well and get things where they are used.

I do *not* advocate putting new storage cabinets

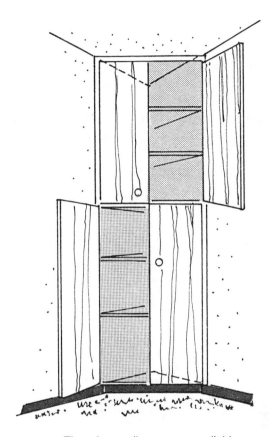

There is usually a corner available for a new storage cabinet.

in every empty space. A space crowded with poorly placed cabinets creates the worst kind of clutter. It's visual clutter that you can't get away from, and it is permanent! Add cabinets with an eye to design.

OUTSIDE STORAGE

Storage needs don't go away on the outside. A woman in New Jersey expressed it this way: "If I were building a house, I would have a three car garage for mower, wheelbarrow, etc." Among other things, this statement points to the need for *convenient* outside storage, with access directly from the house.

Garage

What doesn't fit in the house ends up in the garage. Some garages are so full there is no room for the cars. When that happens, you can either change your habits or build another garage for the cars.

Another solution is to *organize* the garage interior for maximum storage with car space included. Throw away the junk and a garage sale will take care of the remainder.

Since the garage usually if *part of the home*, treat it that way and it won't be a cluttered place. Here are a few ideas:

1. Organize storage as you would for inside space, making the best use of walls and closets.
2. Check do-it-yourself stores for storage racks, hooks, peg boards, hangers, bins, shelving, etc.
3. Use cabinets for items that should be kept dust free. Label the doors so you know what is there.
4. If non-bearing walls are frame construction, between the studs is good space for small tool storage.
5. Overhead racks should be constructed with care for structural soundness and the safety of people below them.

Other Options

Outside storage often means things piled against a wall somewhere. Better options include adding storerooms and planning space under decks, porches, stairs, etc. (for noncombustible items). It depends upon your own situation, but remember . . . organize! NOTE: If an enclosed area (such as under decks, porches, or stairs) is designated for storage, have a fireproof material applied to the inside surfaces.

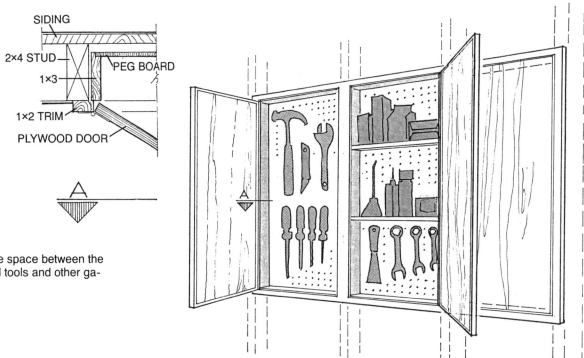

SIDING

2×4 STUD

1×3

PEG BOARD

1×2 TRIM

PLYWOOD DOOR

A

A

Cabinets in the space between the studs for small tools and other garage items.

REMODELING AND ADDITIONS

I have been talking about adding storage in existing space without actual renovation taking place. If you do remodel or add on, the opportunities greatly increase.

With renovation you can make your home easier to clean, maintain, and manage, and more pleasant to live and work in, while customizing all storage requirements. My book, *Discover Your Dream House*, includes check list methods used to accomplish that goal.

GENERAL STORAGE WITH FLEXIBLE SPACE

Place storage around the house for specific items where needed. Then consolidate *general* storage in one large closet. With new construction, or when remodeling, I like to include at least one large closet, about 6' by 10' to 12'. If well organized, it's an ideal place to consolidate possessions. Also, you don't have to remember in which part of the house you put something three years ago.

Resistance to a large closet is common. It's a big chunk out of a plan, just for storage, but a lot of small spaces use as much square footage. Also, many cabinets and closets, with doors and hardware, are costlier to build.

Use both types of spaces. You will be glad to have a large "general" storage space, and scattered storage has advantages for "getting at things quickly, where you need and use them."

AND THE PUBLIC KEEPS BUYING IT

A question I have asked hundreds of women is "What are the most irritating areas of your home?" *Lack of storage*, or poor storage, is the most frequent answer!

An example was the response of many women living in older housing: "Small closets."

New housing offers storage, but not enough for a growing family. We have more *things* than we used to have. In new housing, poor storage is described differently — "not enough closets."

Only a small fraction of all housing is custom designed for specific people. Even then many have small closets and poor storage. So, who is to blame? The blame is as universal as the problem.

Let's remember that housing with "small closets" and "not enough closets" keeps being built by developers and sold to the public. It's like the excuse given for bad TV programs. "The public keeps buying it." So, speak louder for functional design where it's needed! Insist on good storage space.

STORAGE BONUS

A woman in Colorado was asked, "What features of your home give you the most pleasure?" She answered, "Spacious, easy to care for with lots of convenient storage." This comment has a message that can be called an *absolute*. One feature depends on the other for success. "Lots of convenient storage" is a *requirement* if you want a "spacious, easy to care for" home.

9
Bedrooms and Bath

A woman told me, "I've locked myself in the bathroom just to have quiet time alone." That is an extreme case and, I hope, not yours. But it does point up an increasing function of the bathroom area as a place of refuge. I am sure that isn't the reason for the popularity of bath remodeling, but it's certainly a by-product.

Studies have shown that bathroom improvements are one of the better investments. So, if your bath-dressing area needs more of everything, and you can afford to do it, there is no excuse to put it off.

BATH-DRESSING AREA

Both sexes benefit from a generous bath-dressing area, but especially women.

Whether you are luxuriating in your private spa with hot water pulsating, or enjoying the benefits of a well-lighted space for makeup and dressing — it's a time and place to relax.

The personal time may be only fifteen (important) minutes. Its brevity only accents the need for pleasant surroundings. Selection of colors, textures, lighting, and fixtures should be done with care.

STORAGE

Usually you can greatly improve storage of all kinds — hanging, drawers, shelves, racks, etc., within the existing space. The bedroom-bath-dressing area offers more opportunities for creative storage than any other, except possibly the kitchen.

Granted, there are limits to how much you can do in a given space without adding on. Let's see how far we can stretch those limits. Also, when creating more storage, be thinking of ways to make *everything* more convenient.

Convenient storage came to mind for a California woman when asked what feature of her home provided the most benefit: "Enough storage in each area for getting things quickly, where you need and use them." And, "Bedroom and dressing area arranged to see clothes and accessories easily — know at a glance what's there."

A New Mexico woman is not so lucky: "It drives me nuts to pull out a blouse that I already ironed and it's a mess because it's crammed in."

Closets

Without great cost, you can create more and better storage in any wardrobe closet.

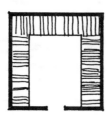

ORIGINAL Walk-in closet with wasted space.

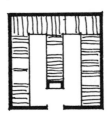

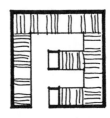

ALTERNATE NO. 1   ALTERNATE NO. 2   ALTERNATE NO. 3

Each of these alternate closet plans
will provide more hanging and storage than the original plan.

CLOSET   CLOSET   CLOSET

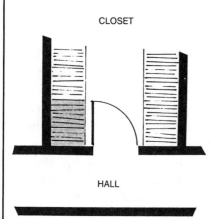

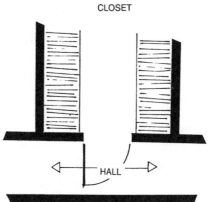

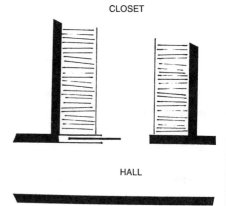

HALL   HALL   HALL

Door swings in and blocks access   Door swings out and blocks hallway   Pocket door is out of the way when
to some clothing. Poor solution.   traffic. Poor solution.   open. Best solution.

The first step is to go through each closet. Decide what you can do without and give it away! Then decide what should be hung and what should be stored flat.

By redesign, you may add enough capacity, in existing closets, to handle your wardrobe. Carefully subdivide the volume for maximum use of the space. A few methods are: (1) create more hanging space with high and low rods; (2) redesign and increase shelving to decrease unused space between shelves and create storage to size for shoes and accessories; (3) look for "closet organizers" (usually coated wire components); coated wire shelving pieces help with cleaning because they don't collect dust; (4) other options include clothes hangers grouped in tandem that also drape vertically (one under the other) for space saving; (5) many walk-in closets are square shaped with much wasted space in the center; draw them to scale and redesign the space for maximum use.

For best results you may have to remove all shelving and rods and redo the closets from scratch. Usually, that is no big job because most closets don't have many shelves and rods.

If your closets have swing-type doors, use the inside face for accessory storage. (Extra hinges on the door might be needed.) A swing door, however, can be wrong for many closets. Swinging out it can be in someone's way and swinging in it hides part of the clothes.

A pocket-type door will solve that problem. Often, wardrobe closet doors are not closed anyway. Pocket doors in that situation are ideal.

I like an air supply duct going to each wardrobe closet. This feature, omitted from many homes, can make a big difference in freshness of clothes, and the closet, generally. Air conditioning is nice, but air circulation is what is needed, so good ventilation alone is a step up from the average.

A storage wall should be customized to your needs for efficient use of space.

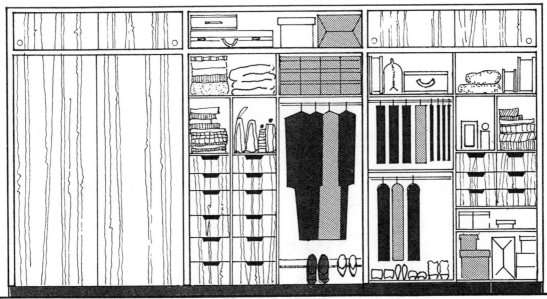

HANGING CLOSET

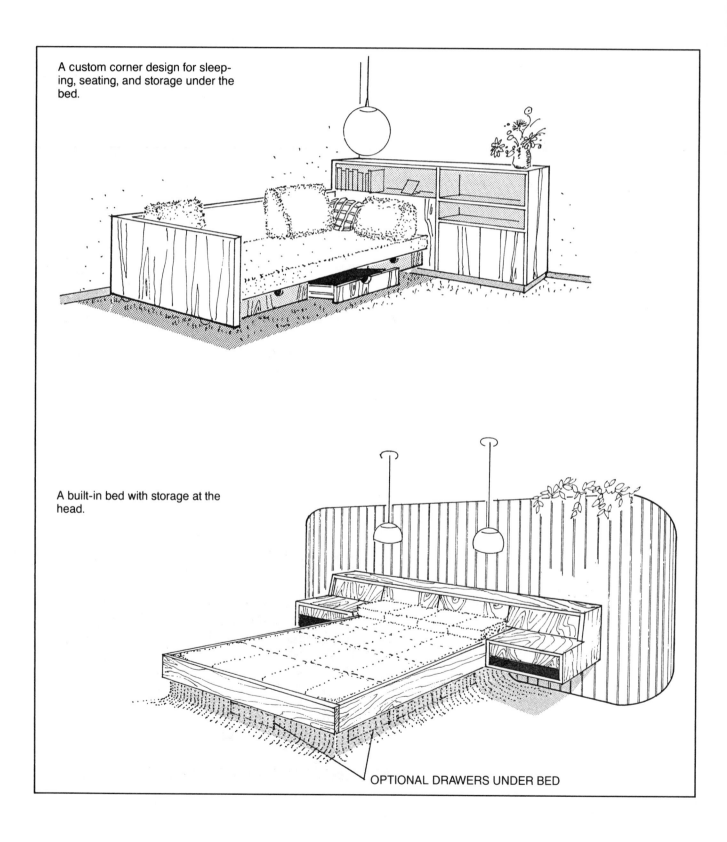

A custom corner design for sleeping, seating, and storage under the bed.

A built-in bed with storage at the head.

OPTIONAL DRAWERS UNDER BED

Bedroom Storage

The bed, the largest piece of furniture, is usually the starting point for room and furniture layout. It's also a good candidate for storage.

Under bed space will hold a lot of storage. It requires custom bed construction with pull-out drawers. Accessory storage at the headboard area is common. See the illustrations for variations.

Other ideas for storage within furniture are mentioned in the Storage chapter.

Bathroom Storage

Most bath areas need more storage than they have. Illustrations shown here may give you thoughts to increase *your* bath storage.

A hamper will fit under the sink if space is allowed for the plumbing.

KEEP FACE OF CABINET BEHIND
FACE OF WATER CLOSET TANK

Extra bath storage in a shallow cabinet above the water closet.

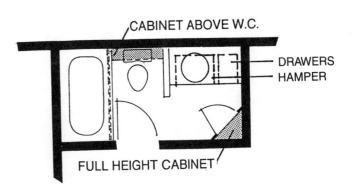

Adding storage in an existing bath.

CABINET ABOVE W.C.

DRAWERS
HAMPER

FULL HEIGHT CABINET

GIMMICKS

Items that make your home a more fun place to be are always worth considering, and many are worth having. A jacuzzi, sauna, exercise area, swimming pool, central vacuum, self-cleaning oven, and home computer are among those popular, and with good reason.

Many items, now standard, may have been first thought of as gimmicks. Such things that come to mind are: garage door opener, microwave oven, and electric can opener.

On the other hand, some ideas may never become "standards" of convenience. Consider the revolving clothes rack. A revolving clothes rack is an okay gimmick, but it has its limitations. For the fun in watching clothes come and go, you lose the advantage of seeing more clothes at one time, which means difficult selection and coordination. And, in case of mechanical or electrical failure, the blouse you wanted might be stuck somewhere out of reach!

I have yet to find a busy woman much interested in household gimmicks to make her life interesting unless the same gimmick also makes her house more fun to be in or maintenance free.

I have no real objection to gimmicks and toys. We all have our share. In home design, however, they are not worth their weight if they don't improve your life.

SMALL BEDROOMS

"The bedrooms are too small!" I have heard it often. Aside from a cramped feeling, there is no place to put things. That means clutter and more work.

Assuming you can't expand the rooms, what can be done within the spaces? Creative furnishing is one option.

Problems of a small bedroom often are compounded by poor location of openings into the room. Sometimes a door can be moved slightly, along the wall, allowing better placement of furniture.

The smallest bedrooms are usually given to the children. Let's look at ways to improve their space.

Storage drawers under a child's bed.

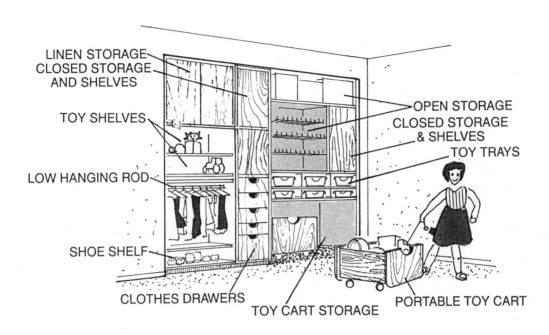

LINEN STORAGE
CLOSED STORAGE
AND SHELVES

TOY SHELVES

LOW HANGING ROD

SHOE SHELF

OPEN STORAGE
CLOSED STORAGE
& SHELVES
TOY TRAYS

CLOTHES DRAWERS

TOY CART STORAGE

PORTABLE TOY CART

Customize a child's room for their very different storage needs.

A Child's Room

The common problem is described by a California woman in this way: "Bedrooms are consistently too small — no storage areas, etc. A child's bedroom furniture is all that will fit. Where do you put the toys, books, and other junk a child collects?"

Children's storage needs are different, yet their bedrooms and closets are always smaller versions of adult spaces.

A good place to start improving a child's room is to take the closet doors off and rebuild the space inside. Children's clothing needs are less than adults. More space is needed, though, for toys, games, sporting gear, junk, and treasures. All built-in storage, cabinets, and shelving that is provided will be used.

Child-sized furniture makes sense. A child's bed is naturally smaller, leaving room for storage furniture and, hopefully, an area for play. (There is a down side, of course, when the children grow up certain furniture may no longer fit them.) Dresser, desk, chair, all can be smaller and still work well. Upper wall cabinets can hold a lot and still leave the floor open. (Have them made and installed by an expert, for safety.) Unused corners can hold small, full height storage cabinets.

When a room is exceptionally small, you might resort to cabinets partially recessed within a stud wall. By that I mean to recess the back portion of the cabinet into the space between the studs. Then, if the cabinet is ten inches deep, only six to seven inches will project into the room.

The bottom line is: if more effort goes into improving the small bedrooms, you will spend less time picking up clutter.

The Bath

Children's bath areas need the same attention to efficient and pleasant design that goes into the master bath. Combine good storage, lighting, colors, and fixtures with easy-to-clean surfaces.

BEDROOM LOCATIONS

A good and workable relationship of bedrooms, to each other and to other spaces within the home, is important for family harmony. As families change, so do room arrangement needs. Let's look at options for location of bedroom areas.

Master Bedroom

Some parents want all bedrooms in a cluster for ready access to the children's rooms. Others prefer the master bedroom separated for more privacy and less noise.

Review your habits and ask yourself some questions. For example: 1) How often, during the day, do you want access to the master bedroom? 2) Is there a physical problem with using a stairway? 3) If the bedroom is upstairs, should you add a small refrigerator, coffee maker, blender, etc.? 4) Do you want an at-home office or reading nearby? 5) Would you like access to an outside deck, court, or pool area?

These are things to consider whether building a new home or remodeling.

Master Bedroom Relocation in an Existing Two Story House

If there is no need for the master bedroom to be upstairs — other than habit — consider a change. How many trips a day do you make up those stairs? How much time and effort can be saved by putting the master suite on the first floor?

If you would benefit from the change, don't rule it out — CHECK IT OUT. The extent of such a revision will vary with each house. It might mean an addition, or readjustment of spaces, or a little of both.

A benefit to the move, beyond convenience, is to have the master bedroom area you've always wanted. Now is your chance to create space, good closets, accessory storage, and *atmosphere*. Include a reading/sitting area if you wish and maybe access to an outside court, deck, or pool area.

Guest Bedroom

For cost effective planning, today's guest room is more likely a multi-purpose space. The *dominant* use among the multi-purpose functions probably will dictate the room location within your home.

If guest room location is based on *convenience* for guests as well as family, then consider the following:

1. Locate the guest room so that guests can come and go without interfering with family functions.
2. The room is best located away from other sleeping areas.
3. The guest room requires ready access to a full bathroom, preferably one for that space only. However, a compartmentalized bath can also serve a double function.
4. The importance of the previous three items varies with the frequency of guests in the home.

Under-furnishing the room has several things going for it: 1) A room cluttered with your personal trappings may not feel comfortable to a guest; 2) A modestly but tastefully furnished room appears larger and more accommodating; 3) A slightly under-furnished room allows space for guests' belongings.

You can achieve an uncluttered look and still include features such as:

1. Cheerful accessories or artwork.
2. Place for magazines or books.
3. Good lighting and a reading chair, if space permits.
4. Full-length mirror.
5. Closet space for guest wardrobe.

I have known people who limit guest closet/ storage space in proportion to the length of time they want guests to stay. I'm not sure if that works or not.

THE WORKING COUPLE

A married ''working woman'' usually means you are a working couple. A couple working the same hours, getting up at the same time, is the true test of design efficiency in the bedroom-dressing-bath area.

Two busy people using the area in harmony means good planning for storage in the bath, and fixtures located to enhance double occupancy. It means good closets, generous circulation between functions, ample vanity space and mirrors, with double lavatories and good lighting.

On the other hand, statistics show that close to three million families have husband and wife working different shifts. When couples don't work the same hours, other criteria are needed for planning this area.

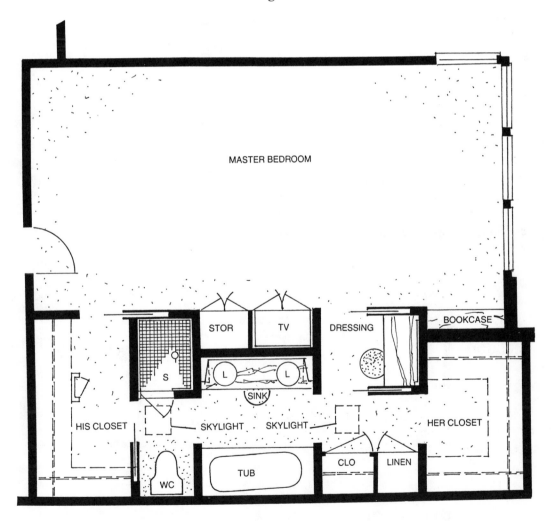

A versatile bath/dressing area for a working couple.

The Split Shift

When he is still sleeping while she gets ready for work, or vice versa, conflict is avoided through design. Isolate the bath, closets, and dressing area from the bedroom.

In this situation, you must have a door for sound control. Around the corner is fine for out of sight, but it doesn't hide the sounds of water splashing, electric razors, radio, or TV. And it doesn't keep reflected light out of a dark bedroom. If space is limited, a pocket door works fine.

Split-shift couples exemplify a need heavily stressed in this book — the need to reduce house-bound chores and increase quality time. It is not unusual that the only time together, for a split-shift couple, is the weekend. That time should not be spent with household "duties" and maintenance. It's a time to relax and enjoy your home and time together.

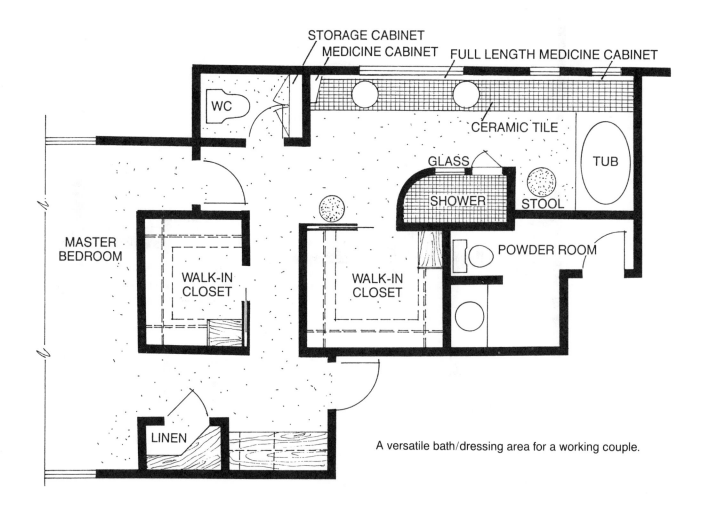

A versatile bath/dressing area for a working couple.

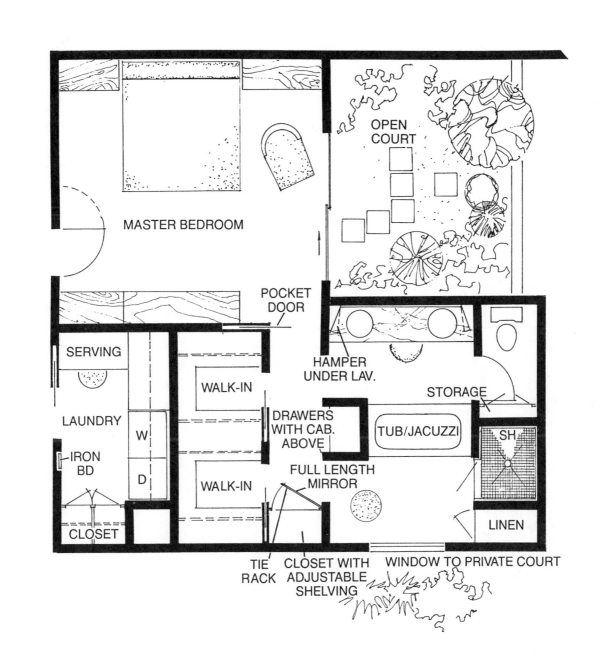

MASTER BEDROOM

OPEN COURT

POCKET DOOR

HAMPER UNDER LAV.

STORAGE

SERVING

WALK-IN

LAUNDRY

W

DRAWERS WITH CAB. ABOVE

TUB/JACUZZI

SH

IRON BD

D

WALK-IN

FULL LENGTH MIRROR

LINEN

CLOSET

TIE RACK

CLOSET WITH ADJUSTABLE SHELVING

WINDOW TO PRIVATE COURT

An efficient arrangement for a split-shift working couple.

10
The Laundry

Busy women of the world — do you really want to buy homes that have the "laundry" located between kitchen and garage, or worse, *in* the garage or basement? Aside from being in the wrong place, it's not a true laundry, but usually a widened hallway with washer and dryer along one wall.

Two relevant comments come from women responding to the question, "What convenience do you wish you had?" (1) "Laundry area next to the bedrooms," and (2) "A laundry room — unfortunately the washer/dryer hookup is in the kitchen. I find the kitchen an unsuitable area for doing laundry."

Let's get the laundry out of the kitchen and into the bedroom area where the clothes are. Some of you may cook and wash clothes at the same time, but I bet you don't dress in the kitchen or keep clothing there. For convenience and time saving, the bedroom wing is the logical location.

If bedrooms are all on the second floor, put the laundry there. If the laundry is on the first floor, you will be carrying large laundry baskets on stairs. And keep it out of the basement! That's two sets of stairs to negotiate.

MAKE IT FIRST CLASS

A 1987 survey by *Working Mother* magazine stated that a large percentage of working mothers iron weekly at home. Almost half of those iron an hour or more each time.

Unless fashion trends swing from cotton and natural fibers back to permanent press, plan on some ironing time. Why not do it in a first class laundry — pleasant, cheerful, and uncluttered.

Uncluttered comes with plenty of shelves, cabinets, and hanging space. Cheerful is a well-planned space with good lighting, nice colors, and finish materials. It doesn't have to be large, but it should be planned to the last inch. Ironing boards can be built in; hanging racks, shelves, or cabinets can be installed over washer and dryer. A sewing machine in here makes clothing repair faster and easier.

ANOTHER OPTION

A Florida woman, with no children at home, had this to say: "Having lived in eight different houses, I have found the best place for the laundry is in the master bathroom! All that's needed is extra storage for laundry supplies and ironing board, etc. I have a full sized stacked washer/dryer combo in a 27-½" square space behind mirrored bi-fold doors and just love it!

"Never again will I go to a basement, garage, or tiny room off the kitchen to do the wash. Clothes come out of the dryer, onto hangers, and into the closet without going through any other part of the house."

A CLOTHES-CARE ROOM

If space permits, the laundry can be a clothes-care room. Included might be washer, dryer, sink(s), closet, ironing board, clothes sorting/checking space, and sewing machine. Have it wired for sound, radio, or even TV if you prefer.

Don't expect other family members to jump on the laundry band wagon. But if you spend much time using the above mentioned equipment — go for it. And don't feel guilty about asking for the best!

A folding ironing board stores easily in a shallow drawer with extension slides.

11
Hobby Spaces

In a survey asking women what function or space they would like to add, over thirty-five percent said a hobby or utility space.

For identification, let's call a hobby a special interest or avocation for fun or profit. A utility room is a space set aside for the maintenance and well-being of the household, i.e., clothes care, storage for cleaning items, potting, etc.

When space is limited, hobby and utility often share a room. However, our discussion here is about spaces set aside for hobby only.

Space for a hobby is a delightful luxury, albeit usually an inexpensive one. Normally, it isn't large, complex, or richly appointed. When hobby space is provided for, it's likely to be used. In fact, the demand may be so strong, you'll be asked to share the space. If that is the case, go ahead and share. Let's see what it takes to make that work.

A MULTI-PURPOSE SPACE

How often have you heard, "I would like to do such and such, if only I had a space for it?" Most of us feel that way, so sharing a space for hobby is common — and workable.

Many combinations of functions can flourish side by side, even hobby with utility, or hobby with recreation, as well as hobby with hobby.

Let's assume you want to create a two-person hobby space. A key ingredient for success is getting the ground rules established.

Objectives

Wife and husband are likely candidates for sharing the space. That is not always easy to do, so be realistic. The trick is to avoid conflict! Defining objectives is very important.

One approach is to pose and answer questions about situations that might occur. For instance:

1. Is one hobby quiet and one noisy?
2. Is one clean and one messy?
3. Does one need a lot of equipment and one less?
4. Is strong light needed for one or both?
5. Are the hobbies of equal importance to each person?
6. Will both use the space at the same time?

Continue the questions until the subject is covered. The space will work well if *planned well*.

A four letter word — mess — is cause for conflict, and some hobbies are messy! Various arts and crafts fit that description. The unique thing about a messy hobby is that the person making the mess doesn't mind at all. But others may not be so forgiving.

Storage as Needed

Storage space is vital — doubly so with a shared space. Keeping the area tidy is possible only with ample and convenient storage for all tools, materials, and partially finished projects.

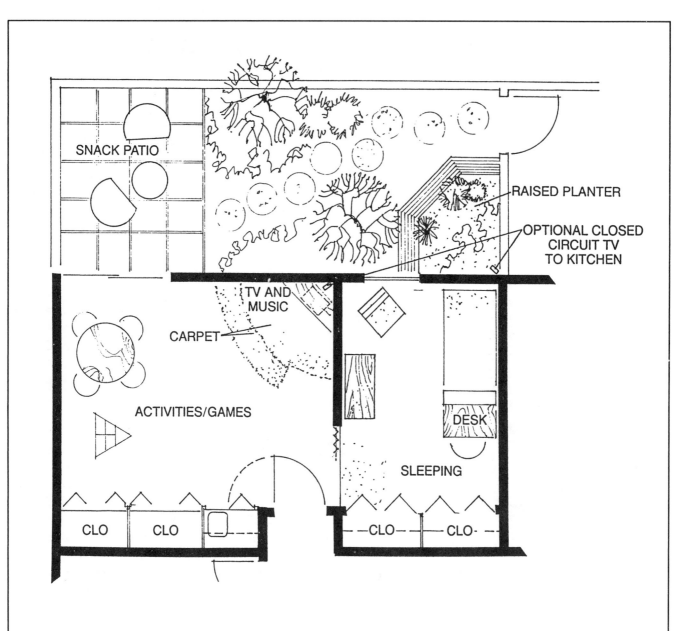

SNACK PATIO

RAISED PLANTER

OPTIONAL CLOSED
CIRCUIT TV
TO KITCHEN

TV AND
MUSIC

CARPET

ACTIVITIES/GAMES

DESK

SLEEPING

CLO   CLO

CLO   CLO

This children's area may be easily converted in the future with small room used for hobbies and
the large room an adult den.

Compatibility Required

After posing questions about conflict, setting the ground rules, and planning the space needed for each hobby, assess the compatibility. If you feel that compatibility is probable, then develop the space. If it seems that conflict will result, plan a separate space for each person.

A ONE HOBBY SPACE

After going through the scenario of a shared multi-purpose space, a single use hobby room seems easy — and it is. Planning ahead, of course, makes it even easier.

Location

If you have a choice of location, select a spot that won't interfere with other household functions. Noise, odor, dust, even vibration can occur with certain hobbies. Orientation for good natural light may be a factor as well.

Utilities and Equipment

Make sure you know the requirements for utilities as well as special equipment. Here are some sample questions to get you started.

1. What custom equipment is needed for your hobby?
2. Must it be built in?
3. Do you have special electrical needs such as a separate circuit for computer equipment?

4. Will the heating and cooling to the space be adequate?
5. Are special exhaust fans required, such as with film developing, woodworking, or sculpting?
6. (a) Do you need special work surface materials?
   (b) Should they be dark, light, smooth, or textured?
   (c) Must they be impervious to cutting or burning?
   (d) Will there be special plumbing needs? For instance: both hot and cold water; a special floor drain with interceptor for waste, as with clay potting.

Storage

Although most hobbies require lots of storage, often it doesn't have to be built into the house. Many hobbies are well served by accessories such as cabinets, bins, adjustable shelving, or devices made especially for the hobby. Portable storage containers on rollers can be especially helpful.

Light and Color

Atmosphere, as always, is vital for productivity and enjoyment of any space. Too often we have the attitude that hobby spaces need only be functional. The opposite is true.

We go to a hobby room for fun, profit, or both. Either way, a bright, cheerful space is an asset. (Photo darkrooms excepted, of course.) Be good to yourself. Provide good natural light, plants, light fixtures, and great color combinations.

12
Special Purpose Spaces

In this chapter, "special purpose" refers to a space set aside for one use only. Your special purpose might be a luxury, like a sauna or gymnasium, or a necessity, like a work-at-home office.

Special purpose spaces may not increase the market value of your home. They represent a different form of investment. Consider that you may live in this home a good part of your life. Think about personalized special spaces as *an investment in your pleasure* that occasionally might increase the market value of your home.

Some special uses that might carry their value on resale are those requiring minimal space, such as a jacuzzi or wet bar.

Exterior features such as a swimming pool, elaborate barbecue/ramada, or a greenhouse, add value to the right buyer, in the right climate. But don't count on it. Build it, if you do, for the pleasure it brings. *Enjoyment* of the special use should weigh heavily in decisions about what to include in your new home or renovation.

SPECIAL PURPOSES

There are certain advantages to having a space customized for only one use, not the least being the atmosphere maintained. For instance, you are more likely to work at being a part-time artist if you have a studio exclusively for painting, potting, or sculpting. With the ideal layout and environment, you can leave your work, come back to it and take up immediately where you left off.

Know the Needs

If you've decided to have a special purpose space, take your planning far enough to know minimum and maximum space requirements. Know what customizing (i.e., utilities, lighting, etc.) is required within the space. Having that information at hand, you can plug the space into the overall design. For instance, a darkroom can be closet-sized or as large as a bedroom. Thus, the extent of your work with camera and film development must be known to set your space needs.

ITEMS OF SPECIAL PURPOSE

Special *items* (as opposed to *spaces*) are amenities requiring little or no space. Many have become commonplace in new home offerings and are usually accepted as attractive features. For some they

An 8′ by 8′ open court opens off the living room, creating a small gallery for the owner's photography collection. Natural light comes through a stained glass skylight.

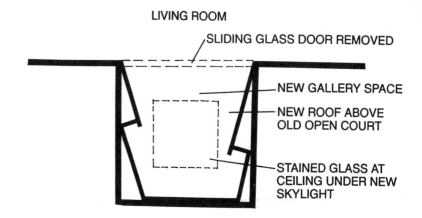

LIVING ROOM

SLIDING GLASS DOOR REMOVED

NEW GALLERY SPACE

NEW ROOF ABOVE OLD OPEN COURT

STAINED GLASS AT CEILING UNDER NEW SKYLIGHT

are requirements. They include built-ins like intercom, sound systems, and security alarms.

Built-in items of this type become a permanent part of the house and often repay their cost at resale time, either in dollar value or as buyer incentives. On the other hand, items such as a sauna, built-in vacuum system, or a partial solar system may return only a small percentage of their cost. Therefore, if built, the purpose should be for your personal satisfaction.

Other special items, such as custom stereo-video cabinets, become pieces of furniture and can be moved to another home.

THE LUXURY MYTH

Luxury is defined by Webster as, "Something desirable, but costly or *hard to get* . . . that few can afford". Good planning and design can rewrite that definition. Many well-done features that give the feeling of luxury and "the good life" are, in fact, relatively inexpensive and *easy to get*.

Also, what one considers a luxury is a necessity to another. In other words, priorities come into the picture.

Know the Cost

Get a realistic idea of costs before making a final decision about special purpose objectives. You may be surprised to find the cost less than expected. (It's equally important to know if the cost will be greater than expected.)

EXPERT ADVICE

Balancing desire with budget is where professional help can pay its way. Creative methods sometimes can be used to affordably get what you want.

Also, expert planning is a must for more sophisticated types of special purpose spaces. A music listening-and-recording room is an example. Other examples could be hydroponic gardening, wine and root cellars, or video theatres. Expert advice may come from a consultant or the study of information prepared by an expert. By whatever method, thoroughly know your special purpose before planning its space.

AN INDOOR GARDEN

Indoor gardening can be the "planted-in-the-earth" variety, plants in pots or boxes, or both. Either way, you must solve the basic needs of light and water.

Natural light is preferred, but a combination of natural and artificial usually works fine. Many plants will grow in partial light. There *are* plants

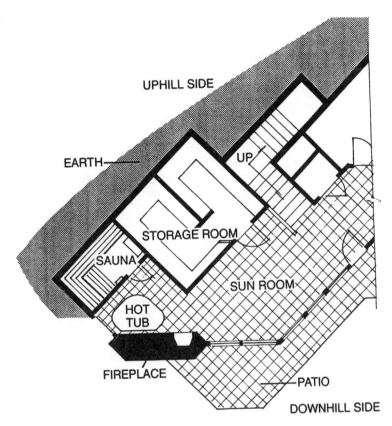

Multi-special purpose–A sun room, sauna, and hot tub in the basement level of a cold weather home built on a hillside.

that grow in near darkness, but aren't much fun if you can't see them.

When planning your indoor garden, discuss it with a local plant specialist. Select plant types ahead of time and get advice about their care, feeding, and light needs.

Planting in the Ground

One advantage to "in-the-ground" planting is the look itself — the natural feeling. Locate plant life convenient to a much used living area so the results of your labors can be enjoyed visually. If your climate does not include extreme temperatures, skylights can be used, further improving the visual effect. If ceiling height permits, you can grow plants or even small trees to a good size, and trees growing in a two-story space can be enjoyed from both levels.

Another advantage is that the ground retains moisture longer than pots or planter boxes so wa-

tering is less frequent. However, water must have a way of draining to keep the soil healthy.

A disadvantage to "in-the-ground" planting is water damage. Devise a means to prevent water from getting under adjacent floors and foundations. An expert should be consulted here.

Greenhouse

A sunspace, doubling as a greenhouse, is a great way to create an indoor garden. A greenhouse is not only fun but offers the chance to grow everything from orchids to onions.

A Gardening Room

A gardening room with pots and boxes offers several possibilities. Plants within the space are nurtured and displayed in a controlled environment. From this room, you can supply potted plants for other areas of the house. One great advantage to having a gardening room, instead of planting in the ground, is the versatility it affords in the type and number of plants. Also, you can replace plants around the house as the mood strikes you.

Your gardening room must have proper floor material, drainage, light, water, potting bench, storage, etc. A lot of "how-to" gardening room literature is on the marketplace.

A Darkroom

Darkroom needs vary with the depth of your photography and developing activity. If you only take family shots, but have a yen to do your own developing, then a converted closet will suffice. However, if photography is a hobby and requires sophisticated developing, a small room is needed. Your planning will include work surfaces, sinks, storage, equipment, lighting, a good exhaust fan and, of course, keeping out unwanted light from adjacent space. Again, consult with an expert in the field.

HELPFUL HINTS

Following is a partial list of factors to keep in mind when planning a special purpose space.

1. What type of floor, wall, and ceiling finish should it have? Must they be hard and impervious, resilient, or have acoustical properties?

2. Will the room be kept neat or messy?
3. Will the space be private or have visitors?
4. How does the function relate to the rest of the house? For instance, how much would the space interact with family room, kitchen, baths, bedrooms, etc.?
5. Should it have private access to outside? Be near the front door?
6. Think about traffic flow. For instance, will it interfere with existing traffic flow to an important area?
7. Does the special purpose require precise temperature or humidity control? If so, it may need its own mechanical system.
8. Is special plumbing or power needed?
9. How noisy is the new function? (Remember that sound insulation is obtained by proper sealing and with special materials, as well as physical distance.)
10. Will you need natural light from windows or skylights?

WHEN TO SEEK HELP

Many types of special purpose layouts benefit from expert help. Don't be bashful about asking other people for helpful tips. Specialists normally are willing to give advice to someone who takes the time to seek them out.

13
Basement Values

There are good reasons for having a basement in all climates. Let's consider its many uses: Basements are used for everything from a fruit cellar to a mother-in-law suite. They are places for special purpose, game room/recreation, or even living/family spaces. Storage, craft, workshop, wine cellar, darkroom, music room, sauna, and exercise area are other common basement functions.

CAUTION: It is thought that radon (a substance in the earth) is more prevalent in basements. Assuming that a certain quantity of radon is hazardous to your health, it is wise to have your home checked for radon content.

A well-built dry basement invites any possibility. However, to make life easy, avoid a function that *requires* you to use it often. Carrying baskets of laundry up and down basement stairs is not my idea of good planning.

In cold wet weather it's a place for activities done outside in good weather — like children's play. Or, as one woman said, "Family room downstairs was great for several children in teenage years with TV located there. Could keep upstairs living room cleaner."

Basement environments are easy to control. They are easily warmed in winter and naturally cool in summer. Hot climate *basements*, or sub-basements, could be economically used in the summer, but they are seldom built.

Note: Care should be taken to have adequate ventilation and exhaust from all basement spaces.

KEEP IT FUN

Basements don't have to be dark and dreary. There is usually a way to let in sunlight. And always install lots of cheerful lighting.

Adding a bath in the basement, when feasible, makes it more livable.

ACCESS AND SAFETY

Don't accept the narrow tread, high open-riser stairs that are often built for basements. They are a hazard. *For safety, there should always be two ways to enter/exit any basement.* One of the exits should be directly to the outside. Insist on good stairway lighting as well.

Exterior Access

An exterior entrance/exit for a basement is needed for both convenience and safety. Options for location depend on house design and site layout. Basically the entrance should be wide and easy. If possible, use it as a way to let in light.

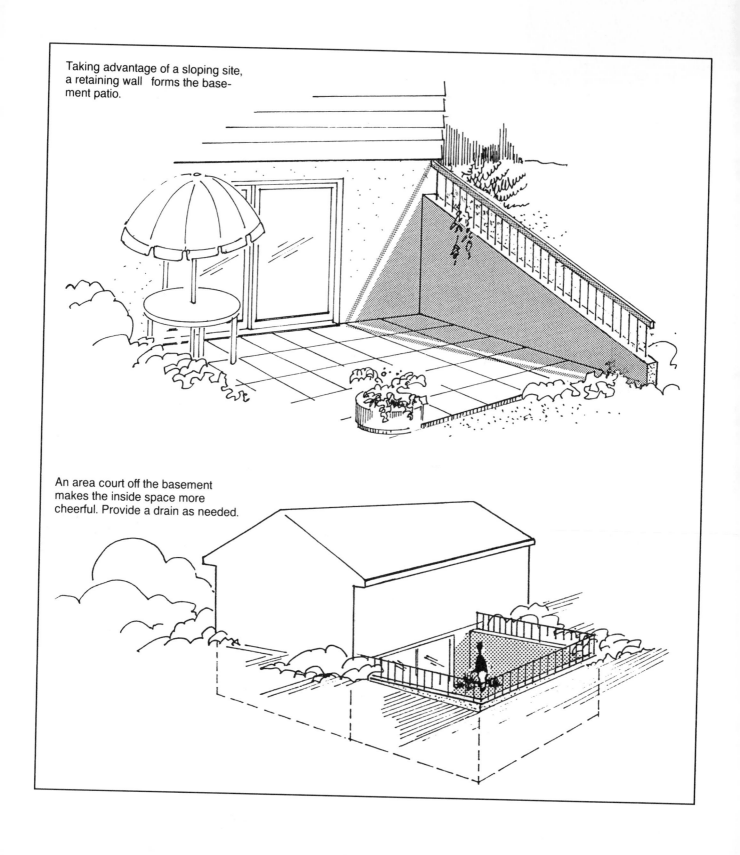

Taking advantage of a sloping site, a retaining wall forms the basement patio.

An area court off the basement makes the inside space more cheerful. Provide a drain as needed.

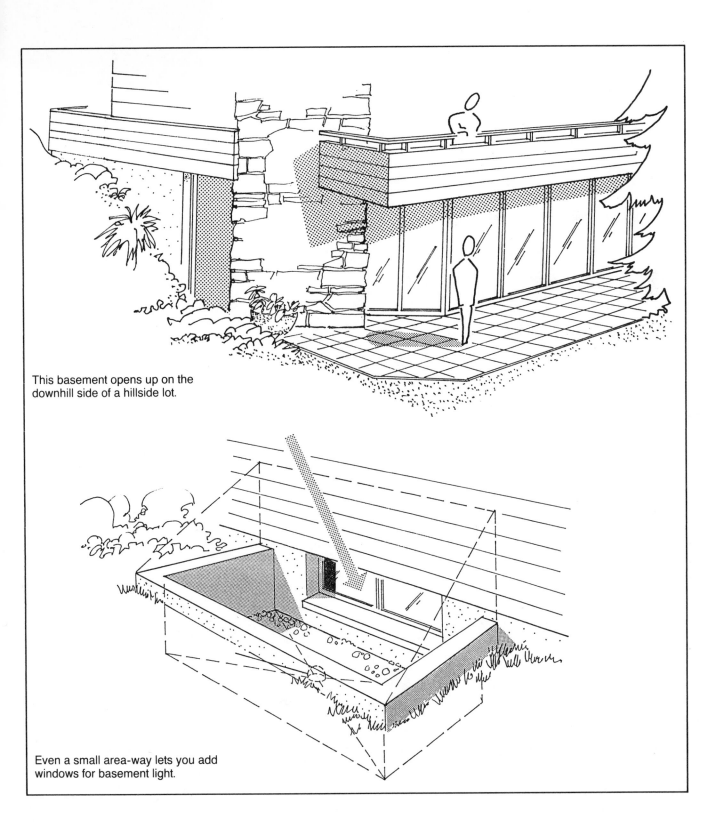

This basement opens up on the downhill side of a hillside lot.

Even a small area-way lets you add windows for basement light.

14
Home Security

Arriving home to discover it has been burglarized must be a traumatic experience. The best way to handle a burglary is to prevent it from happening. Prevention is never guaranteed, but efforts directed to deterring burglary offer a certain peace of mind.

HOME SECURITY CHECK LIST

There is a lot you can do to improve your home security. Listed below is a partial home security check list to get you started. Add to the list, or delete, as it fits your own situation. As I am not a security expert, I encourage you to ask your local police to share with you their home security knowledge.

DOORS AND LOCKS

Doors are made with hollow-core or solid-core construction. Exterior doors should be solid-core.

The outside knob will have a lockset for the latch. However, door knob latches can be forced open. You must, in addition, have a deadbolt lock installed above the knob.

When you buy a deadbolt, look for the following features:

A one inch throw (the bolt extends at least one inch from edge of door).
All connecting screws should be on the inside of the door.

The strike plate should be mounted with screws at least three inches long.
The cylinder should have a tapered or rotating steel guard.

Double Doors

If you like the look of double doors for the front entry, be aware that they are easily forced unless bolts are installed at the top and bottom of each door. Be sure bolts are mounted into solid material.

Hinges

Typically, entry doors open to the inside, with hinge pins inside, and are thus free from tampering. When doors open out, however, the hinge pins are exposed. In that case, a burglar can remove the pins and lift out the door — your deadbolt going to waste.

To prevent this, use hinges with a security stud built in. With this feature, a stud is attached to one leaf of the hinge, and projects into a hole in the matching leaf when the door is closed. Even with hinge pin removed, the door can't be moved because the stud keeps the hinge leaves from sliding apart.

If you don't want to buy this special hinge, you can improvise with your existing hinge to accomplish the same thing.

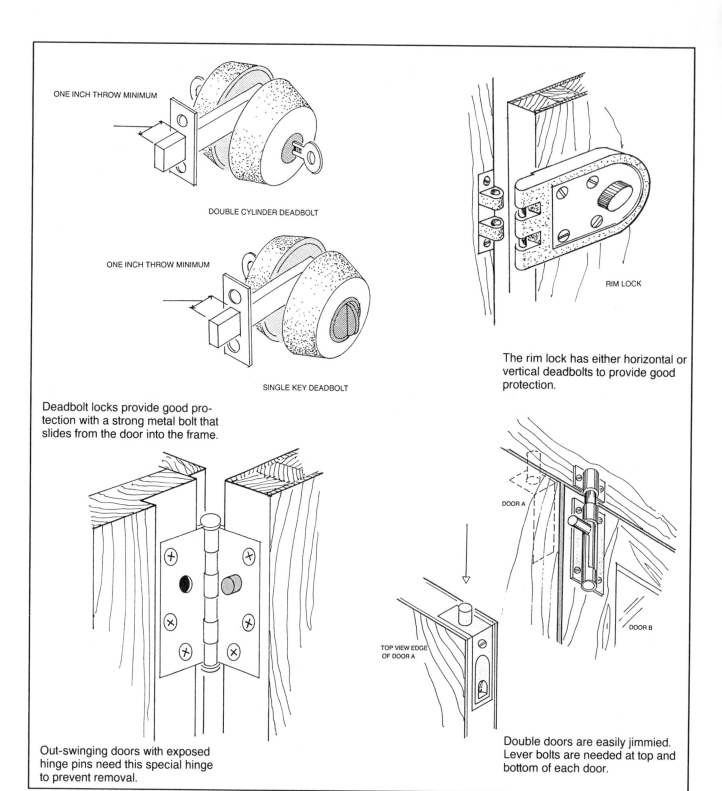

ONE INCH THROW MINIMUM

DOUBLE CYLINDER DEADBOLT

ONE INCH THROW MINIMUM

SINGLE KEY DEADBOLT

Deadbolt locks provide good protection with a strong metal bolt that slides from the door into the frame.

RIM LOCK

The rim lock has either horizontal or vertical deadbolts to provide good protection.

DOOR A

DOOR B

TOP VIEW EDGE OF DOOR A

Out-swinging doors with exposed hinge pins need this special hinge to prevent removal.

Double doors are easily jimmied. Lever bolts are needed at top and bottom of each door.

Door Viewers

Don't open your door without knowing who is outside. Install a through-door viewer. Most viewers have a wide-angle lens to let you see someone standing to one side of the door.

Sliding Glass Doors

Standard sliding glass doors are a piece of cake for burglars. Additional locks are needed to prevent sliding and keep the door from being lifted out of the track (see illustrations).

Windows

Horizontal sliding windows can be given the same type of protection as sliding glass doors.

Double-hung or *single-hung windows* can be treated by drilling angled holes and inserting nails or eye bolts.

Casement windows are easily secured. With window tight and latch closed, drill a small hole through latch frame and handle. Insert a metal pin through the hole (see illustrations).

As an extra option, special key locks are available. I do not like this feature, however, because it

Sliding Glass Door

Drill a hole a few inches from each end of top track to receive a heavy sheet metal screw. Adjust screws to barely clear the track when sliding the door.

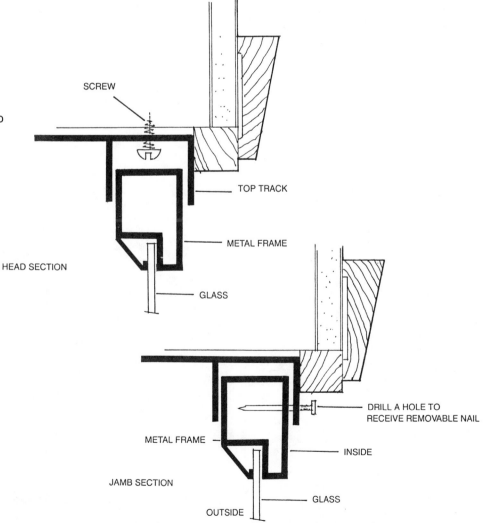

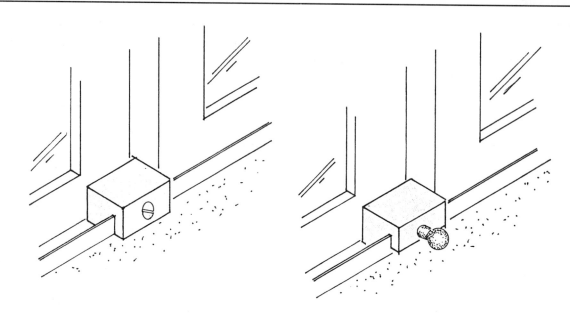

Sliding glass door with supplementary locks.

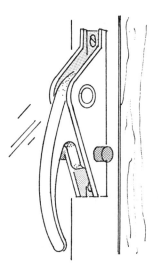

Casement crank windows are secured with a metal pin inserted in the closed latch. Drill a hole to receive the pin.

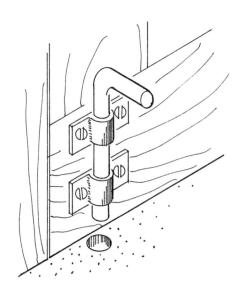

Cane bolt used with garage or utility doors.

may limit exiting in emergencies if the key is not handy.

Some people use ornamental grillwork for first floor windows. Grills offer protection but also limit exiting from the space in case of fire. For that reason, many building codes don't allow, and I don't advocate, their use on bedroom windows.

Louvered windows are nice to use in certain climates but I know of no way to secure them. If the jamb is deep enough, perhaps lockable shutters can be installed to close over the louvers.

Lockable roll screens are also available to cover most window types.

"Other" Doors

Don't stop with front and back doors. Other areas of your property contain valuables, and some allow access to the house as well. Cellar, garage, patios, storage room doors, etc., should all have solid doors equipped with good locks.

ALARMS

Of what priority is an electric alarm system in your home? The answer might depend on where you live. Those who give it a high priority probably live in a high density area. Women living in rural areas are apt to consider an alarm setup less important. I think some type of alarm is a good idea in every home.

Alarm systems are not all created equal. Also, an alarm system should be tailored to your individual needs. Consult with several dealers for price, equipment, and service. Check their references.

Perimeter Alarms

Perimeter alarms are early detection devices, giving warning before the burglar enters the home. Basically, sensors are attached to passageways such as doors and windows.

Electronic and Ultrasonic Alarms

This system, usually installed inside the home, operates by electric "eyes," pressure mats, ultrasonic, or microwave systems. Detection of the intruder occurs after entering the home.

Consult Experts

This discussion is not intended to be the last word in alarms. I do recommend that you consult with alarm experts.

Experts I have consulted express the idea of discouraging burglars from even trying. Part of that theory is that if you make the alarm presence known, they might go elsewhere for easier pickings.

Visible indications of an alarm system would therefore seem to be an advantage. Posted signs and a siren box mounted on the wall are such indications. These items, of course, should be lighted for night visibility. Taking it further, exterior lighting of all the grounds around the house is another extension of the deterrent theory.

When to Install

It's always nice to have the alarm system installed when a home is in construction, allowing certain components to be built in. However, it can be installed at any time, in any home.

Lack of Consensus

I have found differing opinions as to what offers the best home security. A common answer includes a combination of things. When asked in my survey how she rated an electric alarm system, one woman said, "Zero — a dog is better." Of course, there is a dog and then there is a DOG! I have never thought a Yorkshire Terrier offered a whole lot in the way of protection. Admittedly though, since one type of alarm system is a barking dog, a small bark is probably better than none at all.

A Dog Helps

By most accounts, a dog does add another measure of security for your home and peace of mind to you. My information tells me that the majority of women across the country have a pet in the home. Of those who don't, many would like a dog, but feel they can't have one. Here are some of the reasons they have given me.

1. Makes the house too messy.
2. Nobody home all day.
3. No dog door; no dog run; no fenced yard.
4. Homeowners travel a lot.
5. A Los Angeles woman who wants a dog said: "I can't have one because the garden and pool maintenance men have to get into the back yard."

Let's discuss these items and look for solutions.

Item 1 — Too Messy: A common complaint is the mess pets create — dirt and hair on furniture and in carpet. The Cleaning chapter includes tips to help reduce dog cleanup. The basic items are: (a) selection of the dog; (b) facilities for the dog; (c) discipline of the dog — and owners. Most dogs can be trained to do anything that's reasonable. That includes using only certain portions of a home and staying off the furniture.

Item 2 — Nobody Home All Day: This should be the reason to *have* a dog, not avoid having one. A security alarm *and* a dog are considered deterrents to a burglar checking out an empty house.

It's true, not all dogs handle being alone in a closed house, but many do. It's a matter of selection, training, and a little luck.

A dog door, going to an outside run, normally takes care of a dog through the day. A slight negative there is that an average-sized burglar can get through a large dog door. There seems no *perfect* solution.

Item 3 — No: Dog Door; Dog Run; Fenced Yard: Each situation can be changed, *often very easily,* allowing you to have a dog.

Too often we are bogged down by lethargy. We do nothing to solve a simple problem. A woman with three dogs wrote: "Would like a dog door." A woman with four dogs said: "A pet door would be wonderful." I bet it would! All that is required is a fenced outdoor area, buying a pet door, and having a solid door or wall to put it in.

The trick is to locate the pet door where you are able to put a fenced area. It's often difficult, but *almost always possible.*

See the illustration and photograph showing how I solved the dog-door/yard access problem in one home. It might inspire you to solve your own situation.

There usually is a way to get the dog to a yard area without interfering with other functions. (See plan.)

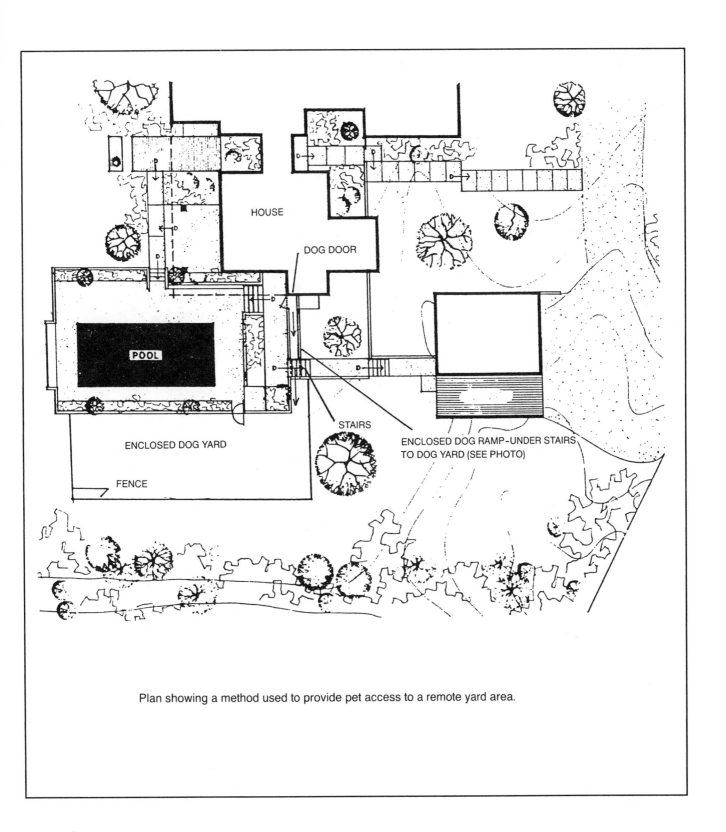

HOUSE

DOG DOOR

POOL

STAIRS

ENCLOSED DOG YARD

ENCLOSED DOG RAMP–UNDER STAIRS
TO DOG YARD (SEE PHOTO)

FENCE

Plan showing a method used to provide pet access to a remote yard area.

Item 4 — Homeowners Travel a Lot: Yes, that can make it more difficult to have a pet. That too, however, is solvable. Here are a few ideas:

(a) Have someone stay at the house while you are gone. That gives you pet care, plant care, and eliminates the burglar-inviting empty house.

(b) Board your pets at a kennel. An obvious solution, but many people are reluctant to put pets in a strange environment, plus that leaves the home totally empty.

(c) Find a well-qualified pet service to come to the home on a daily basis to feed and play with your pets. I was surprised to find the availability of this type of service around the country. Check their references.

Item 5 — Gardener/Pool Maintenance Man in Back Yard: I don't know the particulars of this situation. But it could be the same type as that faced in the illustration for Item 3. Usually there is a solution.

Ask the Police

The ideas noted in this chapter only scratch the surface. Household crime prevention covers a wide area, from "operation identification" to vacation precautions and more. Ask your police department for crime prevention information. Talk to your police department about crime prevention for *your* home.

15
Outside Factors

Many choose landscaping as the first place to spend for home improvement.

My experience tells me that over sixty percent of women get involved with landscape maintenance. Most of you would like it simplified. It can be.

Opinions about landscape maintenance ("yard work") vary widely, depending on who does the work.

For years, when I needed new plants at my own home, I got advice from a close friend, an excellent landscape architect.

Invariably, when asked if the selected plants required much work, he'd say, "No, just an occasional trim." In fact, often they needed constant attention. Eventually, I discovered why he made light of plant care — he never did any yard work, his wife did it all!

Thinking about the outside of your home should be thoughts of the pleasure it gives you. If your first thoughts are of never-ending work, you're doing something wrong.

Let's look at ideas to change the outside from hard labor to fun in the sun.

YARD WORK — LANDSCAPE FOR EASY CARE

Select plant materials that require little care and cleanup. No attempt is made here to write a how-to with selection of plants, shrubs, and trees. Because of diverse conditions in soil and climate, it's best to consult with local experts.

Local Experts

Most local magazines and newspapers have a section on landscaping and gardening. In my experience, usually it's good information.

Selecting a good nursery is the next step. Get *specific* information on plant material. Don't accept generalities. You need to know:

1. How much plant care is required?
2. How hardy are the plants?
3. How much and how often to water?
4. Do they drop a lot of leaves, blossoms, pods, limbs, etc.?
5. How much trimming and fertilizing is required?
6. Are they annuals or perennials?
7. Will the plants take full sun or do they need partial shade?

Of course, landscaping is not limited to plants and trees. There are rocks and boulders, patios, decks, walks, walls, terraces, earth mounds, gravel, ponds, and fountains. Maintenance varies with type of design, construction, and materials selection. Gravel, ponds, and fountains usually do need some care.

Selecting a landscape architect, with an eye to your specific needs, is time well spent. Look at their work. Find one who has created a beautiful, yet relatively trouble-free, outside environment.

Let Technology Work for You

In the survey I asked these two questions: (1) "What time saving features do you have?" A woman answered, "A sprinkling system in the front yard." And (2) "What time saving features do you wish you had?" She answered, "A sprinkling system in the back yard." The obvious point here is that once you discover a convenience, put it to work — in both yards!

An automatic watering system is a time saver, and with a big yard, a big time saver. Time clocks, set to control a watering system, watering as often, and for as long as needed, are the ultimate time saver.

IT STARTS WITH DESIGN

"Master planning" is a common expression and method used in the development of exterior areas. No place is it of more value than the exterior areas around your home. Good design in master planning the outdoor area concentrates on *quality rather than quantity.*

Plan the area on paper first to get the most effect with the fewest materials. Aesthetic pleasure and low maintenance CAN go hand in hand.

When outside space is well designed, each space is carefully considered. The relationship between the areas, one to another, seems complete. Surface treatments, recreational areas, features — plants and trees, courts and walls — all flow together naturally.

Design the Entry

Set the tone for your home environment with the entrance. The entrance to your home isn't the front door. It begins with the first thing visible approaching the house. Whether a drive, walks, yard, plants and trees, or a well done entry court, it's the first statement about you and your home.

More important, it sets the tone every time *you* return there. The approach to your home should trigger the joy of returning to a pleasant atmosphere.

OUTSIDE FUN

If the outside is useful as well as good looking, the benefits multiply. Not the least among them is that outside fun and socializing *are outside*. A livable and well maintained outside area will not only give pleasure, but reduce mess, bustle, traffic, noise, and frayed nerves — on the inside!

Cooking Out

The practical advantages of outdoor cooking increase with frequency. Some advantages are:

1. Less kitchen cleanup.
2. Enjoy entertaining while keeping heat out of the kitchen in hot summer months.
3. It's a good way to get others involved with cooking. The man often does the barbecue cooking.
4. For reasons, real or psychological, food cooked outdoors often seems to taste better.

Locate the outdoor grill convenient to kitchen and eating area. Benefits diminish if the meat gets cold hiking from grill to table.

Cooking over charcoal is the tried and true method, and for the purist, it's the only way to go. My preference, however, is a gas grill.

For my purposes, a gas grill is easier, faster, and cleaner. Those who switch from charcoal to gas seem to use the grill more often. Naturally, basic safety precautions should be taken and be aware that the gas flame can blow out on a windy day.

I must admit that my personal experience has been with natural gas, piped to the house. I have little experience in the use of bottled gas.

Virtually anything can be cooked outside, using either charcoal or gas. With a little experience you will be doing fish, fowl, and vegetables along with the traditional hamburgers, hot dogs, steaks, and chops.

Note: I have no knowledge of the ecological or health hazards (if any) associated with grill cooking, using either gas or charcoal. That is something you have to check out yourself.

OUTSIDE STORAGE

An area designed for socializing needs a place for extra chairs, tables, trays, cushions, towels, etc. Have a large closet near the patio, deck, pool, or recreation area for furniture and accessory storage.

Likewise, if you have a swimming pool, chemicals, brushes, poles, hoses, floats, and miscellaneous pool accessories should be kept nearby.

If outdoor fun centers on games, it's only sensible to have balls, nets, racquets, toys, etc., stored conveniently. When these items are stored indoors, either they won't be used often, or when used they will be left scattered around as outdoor clutter. When they are returned inside, any dirt stuck to them probably will fall off just inside the door.

EXTERIOR HOME MAINTENANCE

Exterior painting ranks among the top ten in frequent home "improvements." I think it's stretching the definition of the word "improvement." I prefer to call it maintenance. The trick with outside maintenance is — *don't let it get so bad that it becomes a major project.* When that happens, "improvement" *is* the right word.

Exterior maintenance is easy to overlook. One day you look carefully and see faded paint, sagging gutters, a worn-out roof and wonder when it all happened.

If your walls are made of colored masonry, brick, or stone, you can get away with neglect. But if they are frame and wood siding, or painted masonry, ongoing maintenance is needed for good appearance and material protection. (It also helps to retain value.)

There are other benefits to keeping up with exterior maintenance. With a good outside appearance you feel good about your home inside *and* out. A well maintained home inspires care to all areas. Landscaping, patios, decks, and recreation areas get more attention and produce more enjoyment.

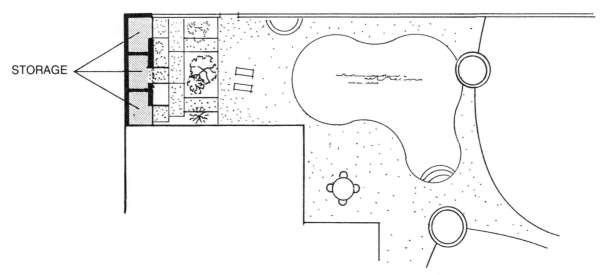

STORAGE

Outside storage for chairs, tables, trays, cushions, recreation and pool equipment.

Reduce the transmission of noise and odor from garage to house.

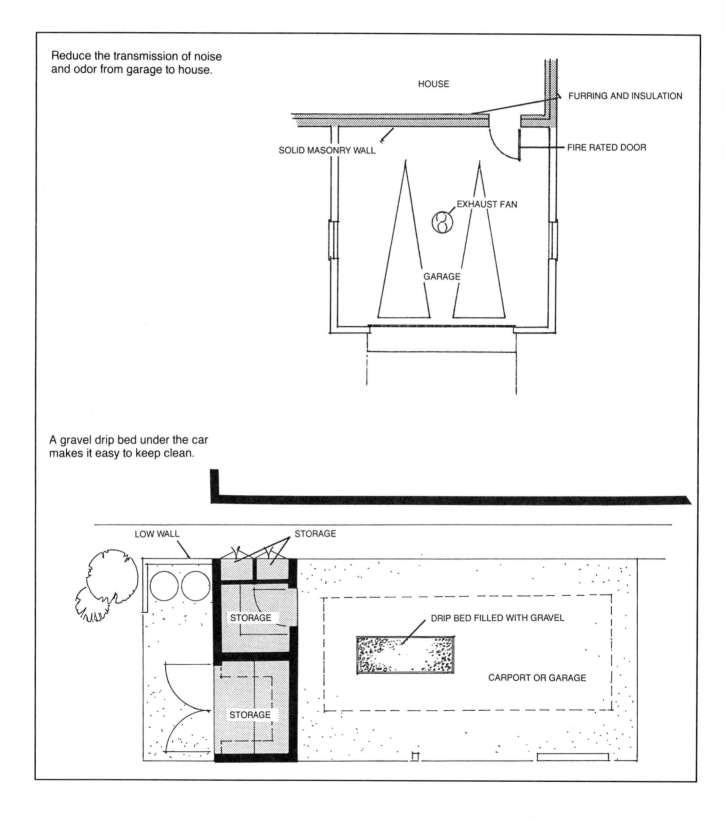

HOUSE

FURRING AND INSULATION

SOLID MASONRY WALL

FIRE RATED DOOR

EXHAUST FAN

GARAGE

A gravel drip bed under the car makes it easy to keep clean.

LOW WALL

STORAGE

STORAGE

STORAGE

DRIP BED FILLED WITH GRAVEL

CARPORT OR GARAGE

The Garage

A woman in Michigan said she would like "A deeper garage so you can walk around your car to the house entrance without pole vaulting over the lawn mower." And, "At least a three car garage (most teenagers have cars nowadays, and husbands collect things)."

Assuming she could have that spacious and well organized garage, there are a few other items to consider.

1. Minimize odor and noise penetration into the house. A solid masonry wall, separating garage and house, is best. Provide a solid core or insulated steel door in this wall. (Check local building code requirements.)

   A strong exhaust fan is a good idea for any garage. Removing engine heat, in hot climates, is one consideration. Health and safety are another, especially with the allergy factor. Some people are highly sensitive to engine exhaust and many other fumes emanating from a garage space. For this reason, living quarters built over a garage may not be the best idea.
2. The floor will be easier to keep clean if the concrete is properly sealed.
3. For dripping oil stains there is an option, but it must be done when the floor is poured. Omit concrete from the rectangular "drip area" under each car. Fill that space with small smooth rocks. The rocks can be easily changed any time you want to remove the oil deposits and have a fresh, clean look.
4. Good lighting is needed. The garage is the wrong place to skimp on brightness.

OUTDOOR PRIVACY

The chapter on Quiet Places talks about the value of outdoor areas conducive to quiet relaxation.

When master planning the outside, provide at least one place for private reflection, reading, or sharing space with another person. There is no formula for such a space. Landscaping, walled courts, sunken pits, raised decks, or under your favorite tree — it doesn't matter where, if the ambience is right.

KIDS' FUN

There is no limit on ideas when it comes to children's outdoor fun. I will mention only two here, each of which goes back to basics. "Basic" means no moving parts, nothing to break or buy batteries for. They do, however, inspire kids' *creative* fun.

The Sandbox

It's been said that the simple sandbox is the most creatively useful object ever devised for young children's outdoor play. I believe it. Without bells and whistles, batteries or video, little ones can spend hours in creative *doing*. Build it sturdy, within view, and try to keep out the neighbor's cat. (Nothing is perfect, I guess. As I finished writing this I read that the Health Research Group, a Washington based consumers group, claims certain fine, white, powdery sand, taken from coastal areas, contains asbestos-related particles that pose a long-term cancer risk to children. So, check out the sand!)

The Playhouse

As children, we had an aunt and uncle, who, having no children of their own, did something to encourage our visits. They built us a small log cabin-type playhouse. It worked. We went there every chance we had. It was simple — a door, two window openings, a table, two benches, and shelves. It had a real shingle roof.

In giving your children a place of their own, you're also giving them something to keep neat and be responsible for.

The benefits are yours as well. You know where the children are (it is hoped), and the noise and mess are kept outside, in a controlled area.

16
Apartment Living

You are right, apartment living is not exactly your "dream house." However, neither does it have to be the poor substitute it often is. Having first made a good apartment selection, there are things you can do to ensure good storage, easier cleaning, and great atmosphere.

THE SELECTION PROCESS

Selecting the right apartment is half the battle. To make it easier, have a list of items that are important to you, and try to get them all. Following are some of the items you might include.

Note basic colors of flooring, walls, cabinets, counters, window coverings, etc. Floors and walls are the surfaces that will help or hinder compatibility with your furnishings.

1. Look for an interior with good natural daylight. The best orientation varies with your location. Ask yourself if you would have good natural light during the time you would normally use a particular space.
2. Check lighting fixtures at ceilings and walls. Poor lighting in living areas can be supplemented with portable lamps. Good lighting for kitchen and bath, however, should be in place.
3. Storage. You can't have too much!
4. Check surfaces to be cleaned, such as carpet, tile, woodwork, walls, window covering, etc. How long would it take you to clean the apart-

ment as you look at it — empty? If it looks like trouble, pass it up. It won't get any easier after you move in.
5. Be aware of the general atmosphere, inside and out, and decide if it lends itself to satisfactory improvements.
6. Security is always important. Look for most of the same things that are important for a house. (Refer to Security chapter.) Security starts with where you park your car, good lighting, and landscaping that is hard to hide behind. Deadbolts and secure window locks are obvious things to look for.
7. General privacy is more obtainable with some apartments than others. Variables are too numerous to list.
8. Check exterior appearance. Building, grounds, *and* management should be trim and neat.

CUSTOMIZING

After finding a good place, the rest is fun. A few ideas to improve livability are listed below.

1. Modular *units* for wall application come ready made, or you can create your own. These units can be rearranged to suit your needs or mood. They hold books, accessories, TV, stereo, art objects, wine and glassware, and general storage. They are available in combinations of open shelves

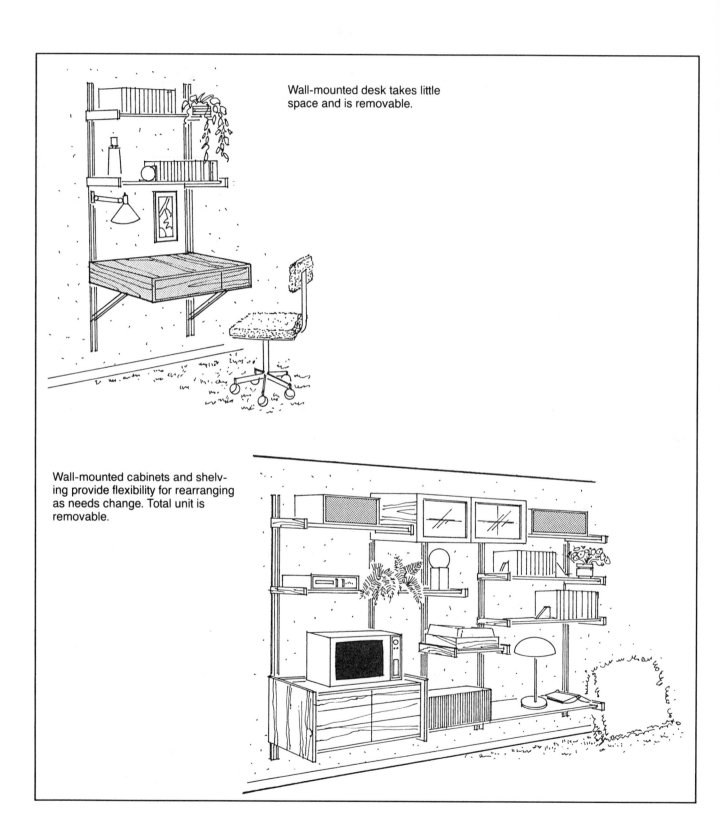

Wall-mounted desk takes little space and is removable.

Wall-mounted cabinets and shelving provide flexibility for rearranging as needs change. Total unit is removable.

and closed cabinets. You can take them with you when you move.

2. *Portable closet organizers* can help make the most of limited closet space.

3. *Wall-mounted furniture* such as a wall desk is space saving and useful. (Permission to mount into the wall may be required.)

4. *Furniture with built-in storage* makes a lot of sense in apartments. Some pieces may have to be custom made, but with ingenuity can be done economically. Bed, sofa, and tables are easily adapted for storage.

Except for exterior amenities shared with others, apartment living is an inside environment over which you have a lot of control. Easy cleaning and maintenance relates to: (1) your initial choice of apartments; (2) your method of furnishing; (3) storage — available and created; and (4) your living habits.

The other major factor, atmosphere, is yours to create. Good colors, texture, lighting, furnishings, and art work — that is what it takes for your own special warm and cheerful environment.

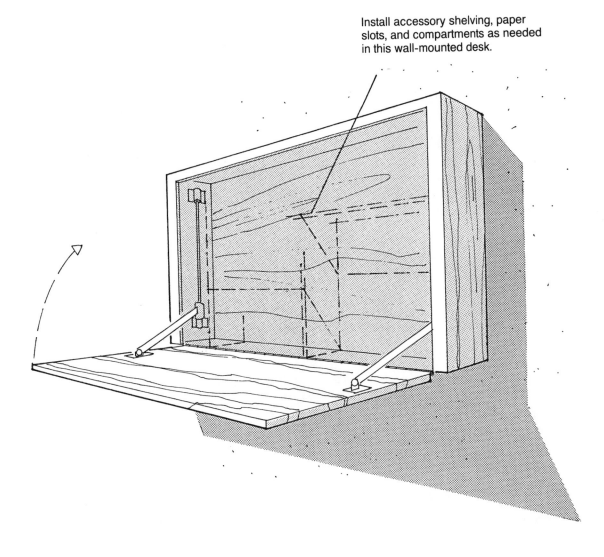

Install accessory shelving, paper slots, and compartments as needed in this wall-mounted desk.

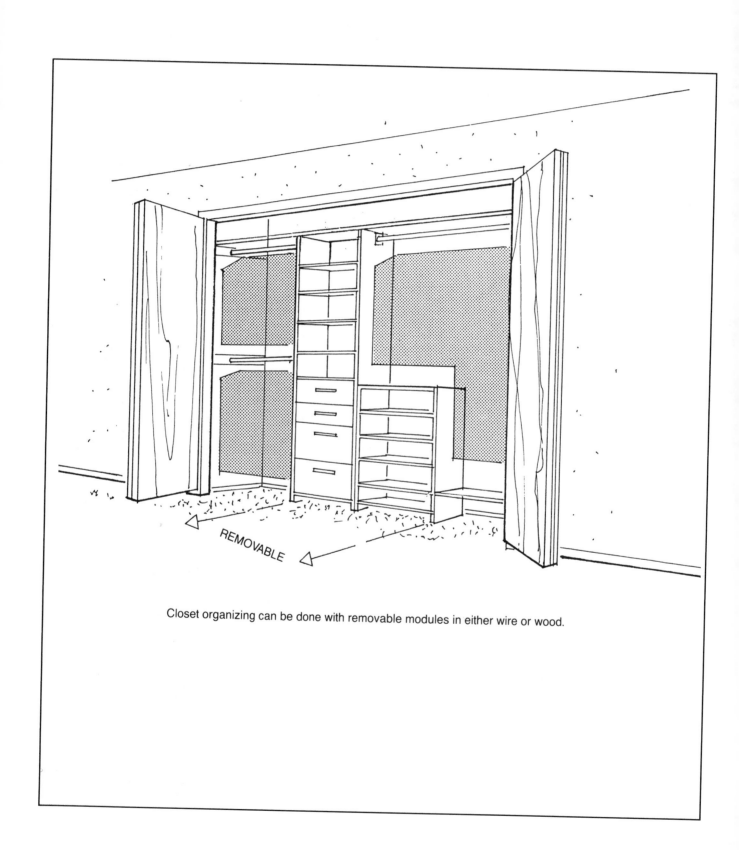

REMOVABLE

Closet organizing can be done with removable modules in either wire or wood.

17
Remodeling — Creating from Within

Your own personal WORKING WOMAN'S DREAM HOUSE may be only a renovation away!

The high cost of land, construction, a new mortgage, and moving may present obstacles too great to buy or build a new house. Okay, put the new house on the shelf, wait awhile. With the right alterations, your dream house *can* be the one you're living in now.

Changing your existing home into the one you have always wanted takes effort and planning, but as I keep saying, you can make it happen! Good direction will help you decide where to start and what to do.

THE PROCESS

The process of home remodeling is one of making decisions. They relate to cost, function, and aesthetics. With good *planning*, you can do more and do it better than you thought was possible.

Most of us have a budget for home remodeling projects. Spending wisely is a balance between economic value and return in satisfaction. Ask yourself this question: Is your house strictly an economic venture or is it your personal sanctuary? Only you can decide how much weight to place in each area. Remembering that your home is your most important environment, begin planning your renovation.

Overimprovement

Overimprovement is possible, of course. However, fear of overimprovement should be tempered by the value of the improvement to your lifestyle. Is the cost offset by the increased enjoyment of your home?

A common guideline is to balance the spending for renovation with the general quality of the home overall.

My book, *Discover Your Dream House*, leads through a process similar to what you would go through with an architect. It presents a method which includes a series of check lists that help pinpoint needed changes and decide what amenities should be added to make your home more livable. With this method you can establish the highest priorities to become part of your renovation.

Here's How You Can Do It!

Start by answering the questions in the Reference Check List at the end of Chapter 1. It's a short list, but it gets you started on the process. The process is to examine separately rooms, spaces, and situations in your home. Ask yourself how each will satisfy your needs, wants, and desired lifestyle.

Perhaps you have isolated your remodeling needs to just one space or function — redoing the kitchen, for instance. Then make your own check list of kitchen features, those existing and those you desire. Describe their location, quality, efficiency, etc. Is your kitchen well lighted? Is it cheerful? Is it a space you like to be in?

Make another list relating to kitchen design. Include everything from floor to ceiling — cabinets, pantry, desk, lighting, storage, etc. The key space in any kitchen is, naturally, the work area. Planning the work area is the most important part of kitchen remodeling. Other functions are important, but they only supplement the work area.

The main work centers — sink, range or cook top, and refrigerator — should form a triangle (except with a one-counter kitchen). Look at your own work triangle. How efficient is it? The relationship of the three functions — sink, cook top, and refrigerator — within your work triangle should fit your preferred method of kitchen operation. Also important is the relationship of the work area to eating areas or to other spaces for people interaction.

Construction Cost

On a cost per square foot basis, the kitchen is usually the most expensive room to build or re-build. Because of the high cost of plumbing, wiring, cabinets, and appliances, kitchen renovation requires careful planning with proper consideration for cost.

Repeat the Process

Use a similar thinking process with other areas of the house as needed to erase your irritations, increase your pleasure, and enhance your desired lifestyle. Explore the exterior as well.

Earlier chapters in this book are intended to help you in that *process*. They include the chapters on Storage, House Cleaning, Convenience, Interaction, Quiet Places, Hobby and Utility, The Laundry, Light, Outside Factors, Furnishings, and Home Security. Each portion is written to assist and improve planning and basic design in home renovation. Use the guidelines and illustrations to stimulate your thinking.

Remember to make decisions based on a direction that will: (1) reduce time spent on "required" tasks; (2) eliminate irritations; (3) increase the quality of your environment and the pleasure desired from your home.

18
Additions

With enough effort and ingenuity, you can dramatically change the appearance, feeling and function of the space within your home. About the only thing you can't do from within is make it bigger.

Or, it could be that you like everything about your home except that it simply isn't large enough. You must either add on or move. You choose to add on.

PLANNING PREPARATION

Adding space to your home means taking space from the yard. Determine what part of your outside space has high priority to remain outside space.

Will a particular outside activity take precedence over a planned inside function? For instance, there may be only one outside space large enough for a much wanted improvement like a swimming pool or special garden. You may choose not to diminish that space for a larger family room or to add a game room.

So, it's important that you first know exactly what part of your yard is the likely portion to build on. Listed below are a few suggestions:

a. Acquire a site plan showing your existing house, garage, storage sheds, or other structures located within the boundary lines. If you don't already have a site plan, have a surveyor do one, or you can draw it yourself. I explain how to do that in this chapter.

b. In most residential areas, you can't build on or next to the property lines. To allow for open space and separation between houses, all construction must set back a certain number of feet from each property line. Check with the building department that governs your area. Read the ordinance which tells you what the building set-backs are.

c. Does your house sit on a flat site or is it built on a slope? Flat lots are considered easiest, but, if you are on a slope, some interesting options open up for you! Depending on which way and how much the land slopes, you might end up with a step up, step down, split level, or two story addition.

d. Does your yard drain properly when it rains? All water should drain away from the house, with no ponding nearby. Suppose you have water ponding exactly where you want to put your addition — don't worry, it's usually correctable. This is a good time to correct a poor site condition.

There usually is more than one solution. Often the ground can be recontoured for good drainage. Maybe dirt fill should be brought in. Sometimes

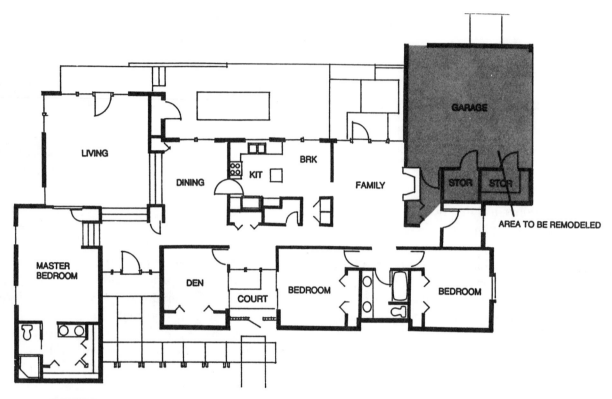

BEFORE   The number one priority for this family was to add a large general activity and recreation space. In addition, they wanted the kitchen/breakfast/family areas opened up for a more spacious feeling.

roof drainage has to be redirected, etc. I advise getting an expert opinion on drainage problems.

Protect the Good Interior Spaces

When planning an addition, it's a happy accident if the logical place to add on abuts an unattractive interior space. You can change the existing space in the process. However, if it occurs next to a favorite and delightful interior space, treat it kindly. Be careful how you create access from existing to new. Be aware of the nice rooms and good spaces and *try not to alter what makes them nice.* That point cannot be overstressed. It's easy to forget that the atmosphere of a favorite spot *will*

change when you: alter the light source, change the traffic pattern, enlarge the space, etc.

The Site Plan

Before planning in depth, have a site plan showing all existing construction on your lot. With the "as built" site plan you can quickly and accurately determine the space available for additions and changes.

With luck, you will have a site plan left by the builder or previous owner. If you strike out there, the options are:

a. Draw it yourself.
b. Have it drawn up by someone else.

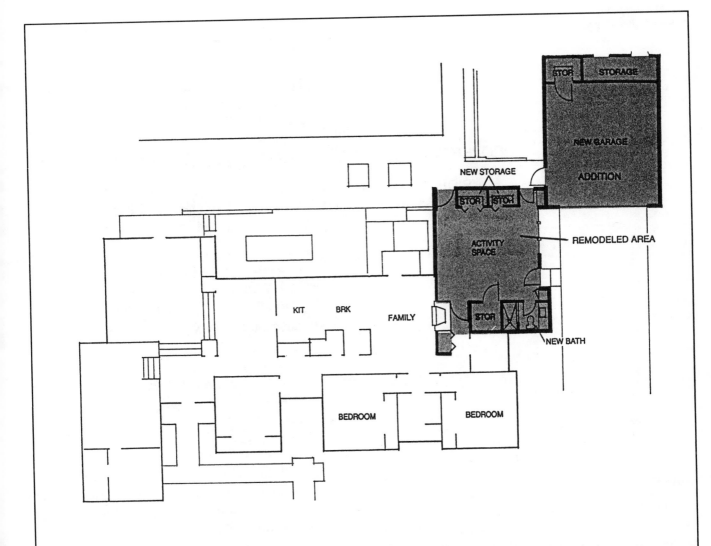

AFTER Traffic flow to the new space is excellent. The space is well located for noise and access to outside activities. Family space is now open to the kitchen.

Sample site plan. Shaded area
shows space available for addition.

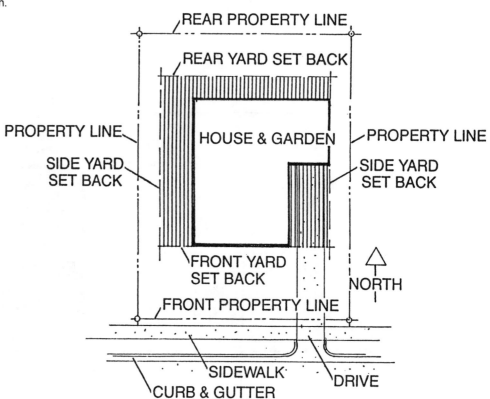

DRAWING IT YOURSELF

Your Property Lines

Finding your property lines is one of the first steps. In some neighborhoods, they are established by existing walls, fences, and utility lines. (Utility lines usually run on an easement that straddles the property line.) Sometimes you can find the corner stakes. Corner stakes, or pins, are normally steel bars about ¾" in diameter driven into the ground with a portion sticking up. (If you are not positive that any found walls, fences, or stakes reflect the accurate property lines, have your property surveyed.)

In drawing your site plan, a convenient type of paper is ¼" graph lined tracing paper about 18" × 24". Select a scale appropriate for your lot size. For example, a scale of 1 inch equals 10 feet means that ¼" on the graph paper equals 2½ feet. Or, at a scale of 1 inch equals 20 feet, each ¼" on the graph paper equals 5 feet. Select the scale that will give you the largest drawing and still fit on the sheet.

Draw your property lines on paper. With information obtained from local building and zoning officials, determine what the building set-back requirements are. The set-back lines are then drawn inside the property lines. The area left inside the set-back lines is for construction.

You are now ready to draw in the house, garage, walls, patios, trees, walks, and drive, etc. In essence, show all existing features within the boundaries of your property lines. A sample site plan and some floor plans are shown here for your reference. More about drawing your plans follows on page 174.

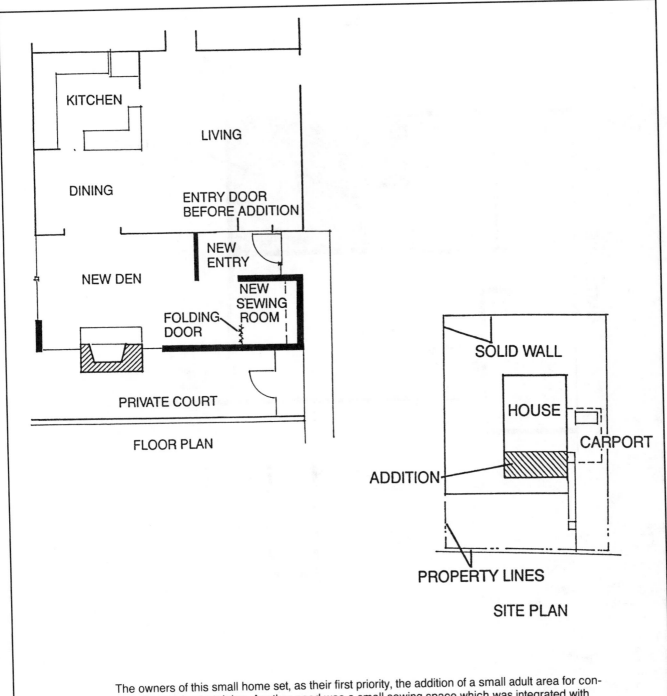

FLOOR PLAN

KITCHEN

LIVING

DINING

ENTRY DOOR
BEFORE ADDITION

NEW
ENTRY

NEW DEN

NEW
SEWING
ROOM

FOLDING
DOOR

PRIVATE COURT

SITE PLAN

SOLID WALL

HOUSE

CARPORT

ADDITION

PROPERTY LINES

The owners of this small home set, as their first priority, the addition of a small adult area for conversation and entertaining. Another need was a small sewing space which was integrated with the design of a new entrance. The addition aesthetically tied in with the existing house.

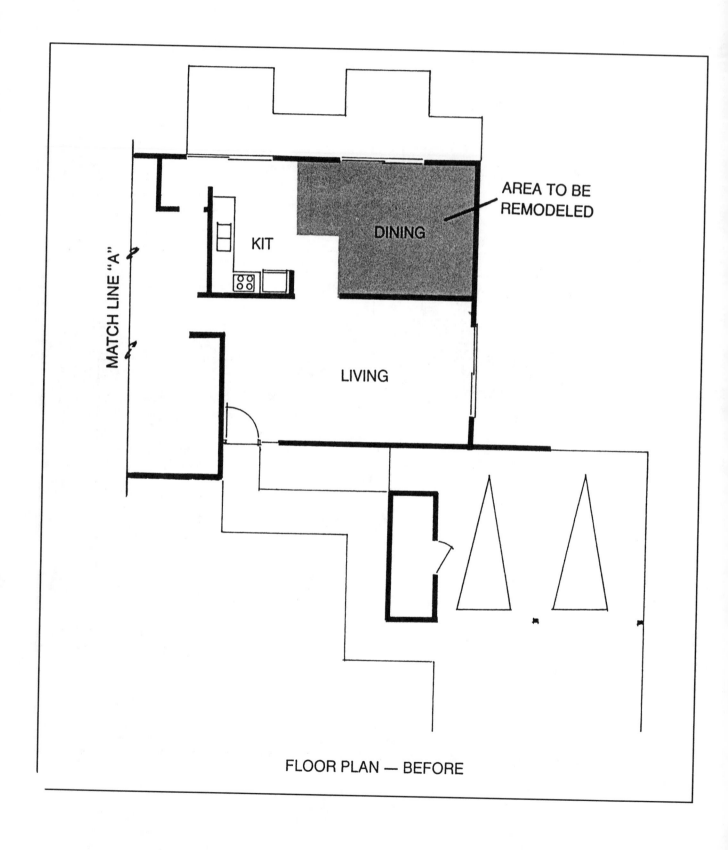

AREA TO BE
REMODELED

DINING

KIT

MATCH LINE "A"

LIVING

FLOOR PLAN — BEFORE

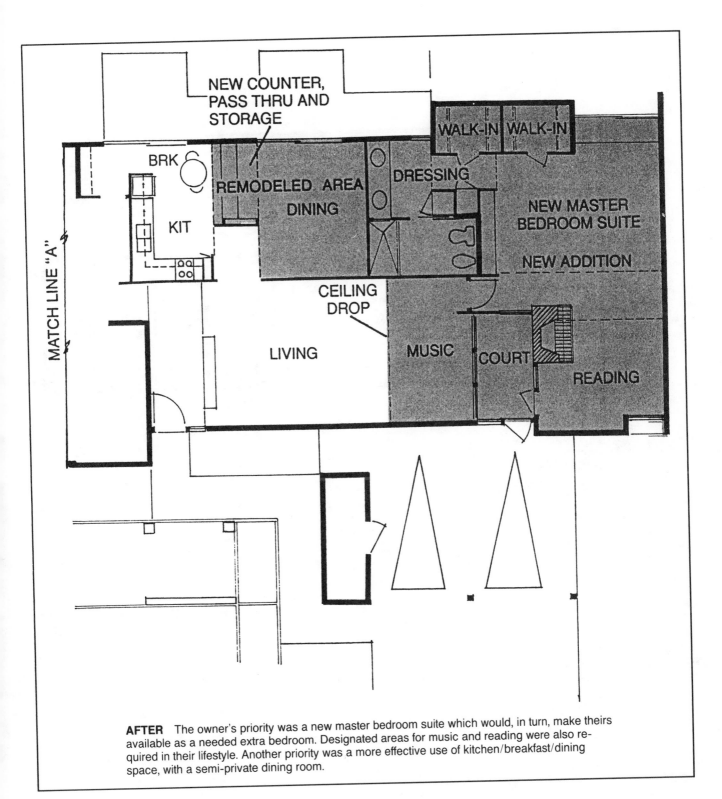

NEW COUNTER, PASS THRU AND STORAGE

WALK-IN WALK-IN

DRESSING

NEW MASTER BEDROOM SUITE

NEW ADDITION

BRK

REMODELED AREA DINING

KIT

CEILING DROP

MATCH LINE "A"

LIVING

MUSIC

COURT

READING

AFTER The owner's priority was a new master bedroom suite which would, in turn, make theirs available as a needed extra bedroom. Designated areas for music and reading were also required in their lifestyle. Another priority was a more effective use of kitchen/breakfast/dining space, with a semi-private dining room.

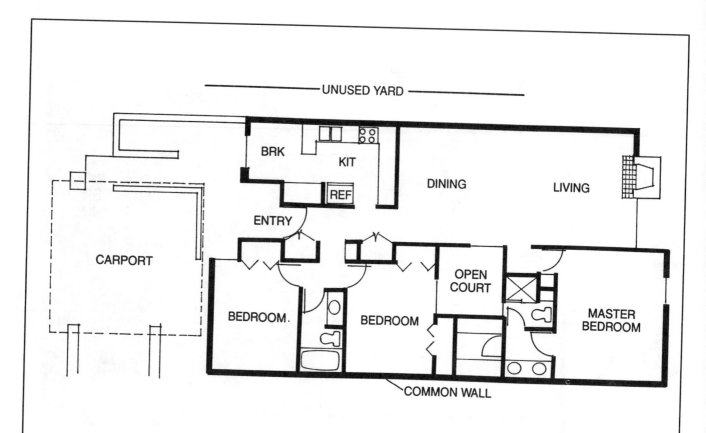

BEFORE   A couple with two children bought this condo on a relatively large corner lot. It contained a side yard that was unused and unseen from within. Inside they wanted a new master bedroom suite, den/office, and revised kitchen opening to a large new family room.

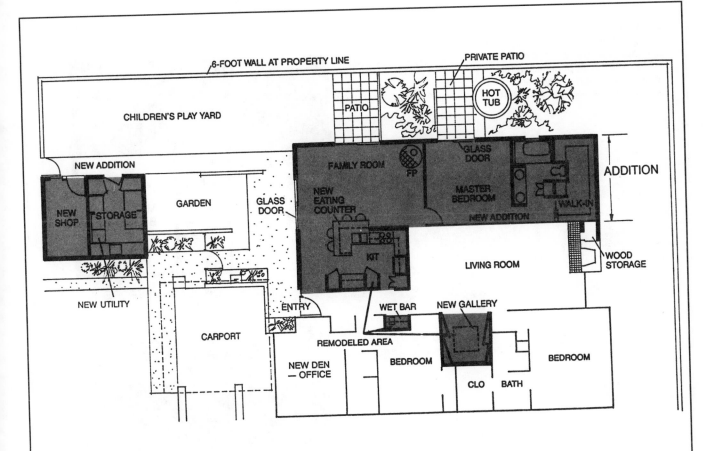

AFTER   The side yard allowed room for expansion. The new space opened up to outside activities. A much needed shop, utility, and storage area was added. The unused interior court was converted to a desired gallery. Each member of the family benefited from the renovation and additions.

BEFORE A young couple, ready to start a family, wanted to upgrade and increase the size of this old home. Their high priorities were to improve the kitchen and bedrooms, and add a master bath and den/family area.

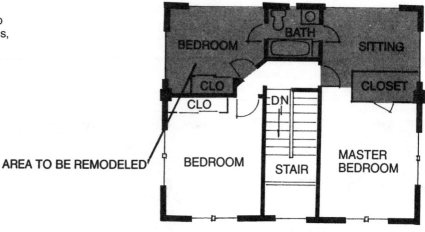

AREA TO BE REMODELED

SECOND FLOOR PLAN — BEFORE

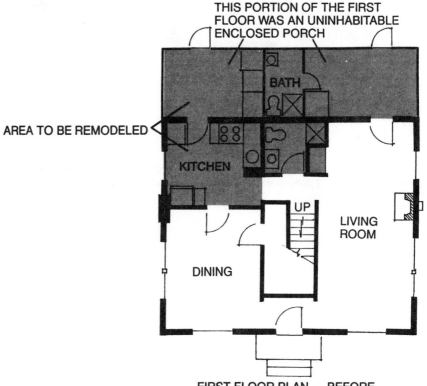

THIS PORTION OF THE FIRST FLOOR WAS AN UNINHABITABLE ENCLOSED PORCH

AREA TO BE REMODELED

FIRST FLOOR PLAN — BEFORE

AFTER Second Floor Plan. Second floor improvements included new walk-in closets, enlarged second bedroom and closet space, a new balcony, and spacious master bath.

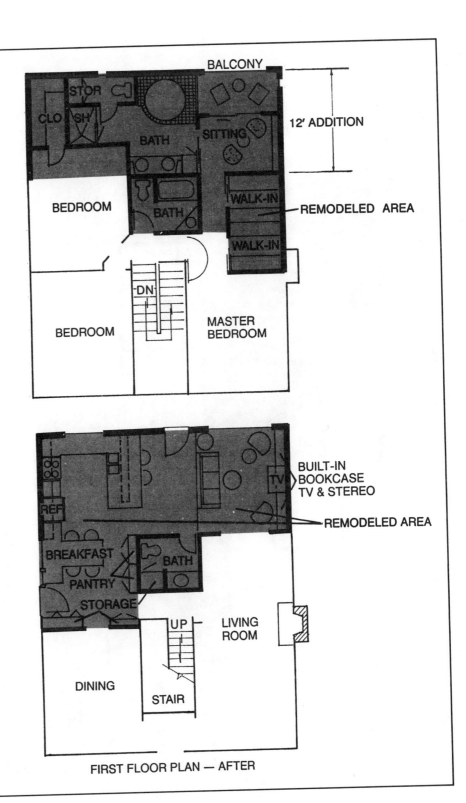

BALCONY

STOR

CLO   SH

BATH

SITTING

12' ADDITION

BEDROOM

BATH

WALK-IN

REMODELED AREA

WALK-IN

DN

BEDROOM

MASTER
BEDROOM

BUILT-IN
BOOKCASE
TV & STEREO

REF

REMODELED AREA

TV

BREAKFAST

BATH

PANTRY

STORAGE

UP

LIVING
ROOM

DINING

STAIR

FIRST FLOOR PLAN — AFTER

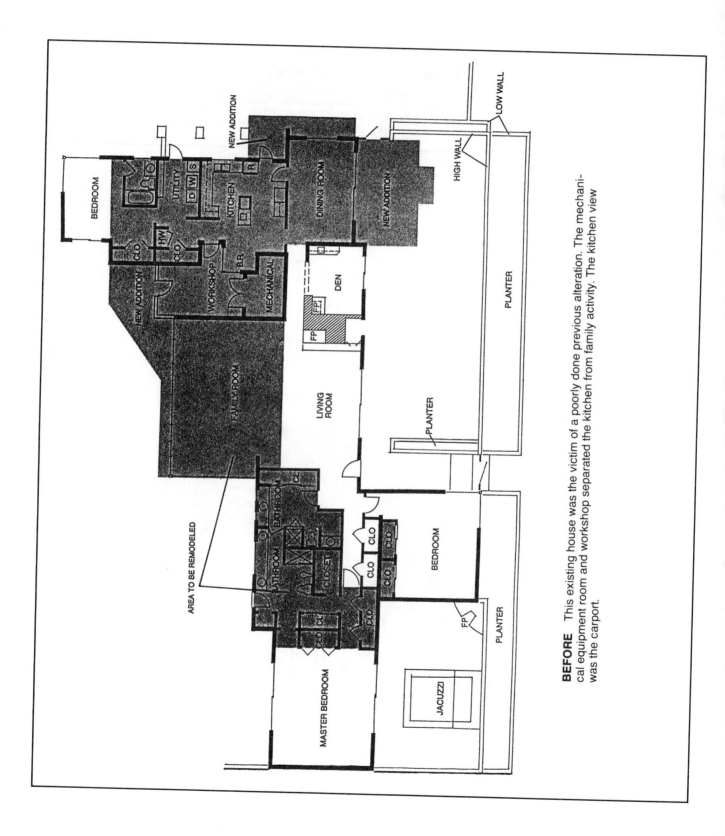

BEFORE This existing house was the victim of a poorly done previous alteration. The mechanical equipment room and workshop separated the kitchen from family activity. The kitchen view was the carport.

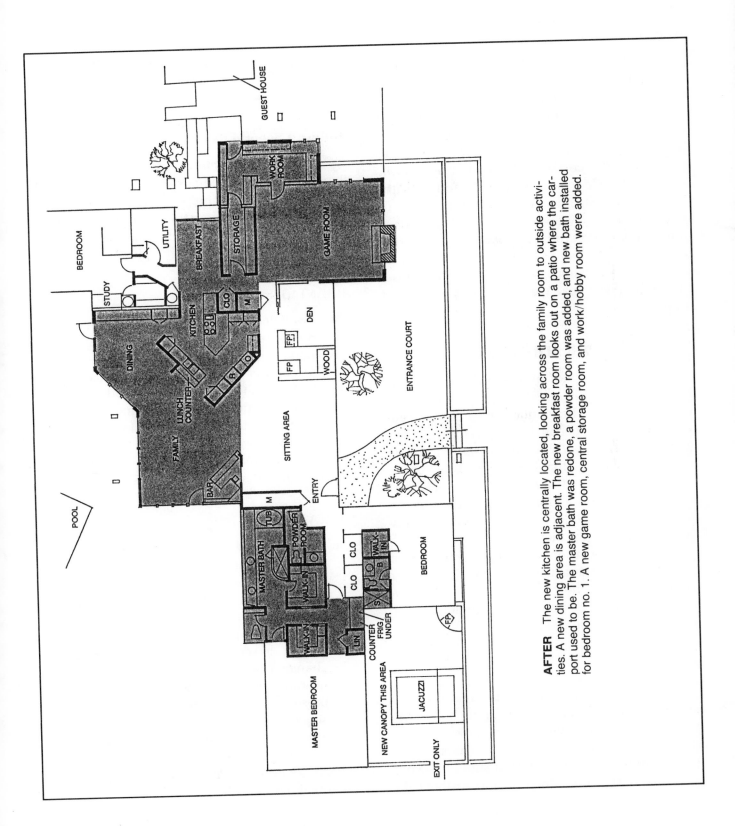

AFTER   The new kitchen is centrally located, looking across the family room to outside activities. A new dining area is adjacent. The new breakfast room looks out on a patio where the carport used to be. The master bath was redone, a powder room was added, and new bath installed for bedroom no. 1. A new game room, central storage room, and work/hobby room were added.

Drawing the Plan

Each time your property lines meet and turn a corner, there should be a metal pin or stake. Run a string between the corners. The string becomes your lot lines. Measure the distance from your strings to every existing improvement on your lot. Draw the improvements (house, garage, pool, sheds, etc.) in the correct place. In this way you will complete the site plan. A necessary caution: Without surveyor instruments you will not be able to attain total accuracy. For *accuracy* you should have your property surveyed and a plan drawn by a registered surveyor. Also, you must determine that no easements, dedications, or deed restrictions exist on the property that would prevent a planned addition.

THE ADDITION

An addition is not necessarily more difficult than rearranging interior space, but it is more immediately visible. The addition must aesthetically complement and become a natural part of the house — *looking as though it was there from the beginning.* Achieving that look is not always easy.

A casual drive through a strange neighborhood can prove the above statement. Look for additions. If they're all done well, you won't find any. Usually you can spot them.

One of the most common is easily, but seldom, corrected. It's the garage or carport which became an interior room. The conversion often looks fine, but the driveway, instead of being re-done, is left running up to a blank wall.

The Natural Look

A well designed addition can make a drab house come to life. Marketability of the home may even become greater. With rare exception, it's possible to design an addition which blends in harmony with the original. In fact, it should be your goal to so design the addition as to aesthetically and functionally *improve* your home. You may need to retain a consultant for help with this effort. If you do, find one with a track record in home additions, and check his or her work.

Adding a Second Floor

A common question is "can we add a second floor to our one story house?". The answer is usually that, with expert help, you can go up, instead of out, but there are more things to consider. Listed below are a few advantages to building new space above, followed by some of the pitfalls.

ADVANTAGES:

a. If well designed, the entire home can become more interesting, inside and outside.

b. Going up instead of out saves space on your lot for other things such as patios, decks, pool, BBQ, recreation, garden, and landscaping.

c. Function can be improved. Some spaces work better with the over-all scheme if isolated on an upper level.

d. Going up may give you more flexibility with design and rearranging space.

DISADVANTAGES:

a. Adding a floor usually is more expensive then adding the same amount of space at ground level.

b. New space must be served by heating and/or cooling systems. Normally, it is easier and cheaper to do it well if all space is on one level.

c. Adding a second floor is a highly visible change. Creating a natural and pleasing appearance requires abilities usually beyond those of the average person.

d. Single story houses are seldom built to accommodate a second floor. Adding above generally means building, or rebuilding, from the foundation up. Professional help should be obtained.

The very first step is to check your local zoning laws and your property deed restrictions. Be sure you are allowed to build over one story.

MARKET VALUE

Additions are a common form of renovation. A well-done addition should have a positive impact on the enjoyment of your home. A word of caution is due, however, about its effect on market value: Additions generally are an expensive form of renovation. It's a rare addition that will increase resale of a home equal to the cost of the addition.

For that reason, if you plan to move in the near future, an addition, in a marketing sense, may not be cost-effective. Some additions, if not well done, can actually hinder resale!

Family rooms and bedrooms are popular additions. Surveys have shown that, typically, about half the cost of construction is added to the resale value.

Adding a full bath, especially in a three bedroom, one bath home, is a better investment risk. It normally adds a higher percentage of its cost in resale value.

A swimming pool in cool climates will add little of its cost to the resale value. In warm climates, however, a pool may return most of its cost on resale.

Reaction to patio or deck additions is similar to pools. Percentage of return is slight in cold climates and higher in the Sun Belt states.

Garage conversions compel another addition — the addition of another garage or at least a carport. While you may not mind parking outside, many potential buyers could be turned off without covered parking.

Garage conversions, with the addition of a new garage, make sense if you have the room to add the extra building. Coupled with adding indoor space is the opportunity to add storage in both converted and new space. In fact, you can take care of storage requirements for the entire home with this particular renovation.

The Bottom Line

Don't count on getting your money back. As with all renovation work, plan it and build it if you intend to stay awhile and want to increase the enjoyment of your home.

19
Building a
New Home

You have decided to start from scratch and *build* your dream house. It's an exciting time! This is your chance to have the environment you always wanted.

What you read in this book will help in your planning. Use the information to help you *get it right the first time.*

Building a new home requires a discipline not needed when buying a home already built. Comments and guidelines in these chapters, combined with your own check lists, will help in *buying* an existing house. Additional items, however, come into play in the *building* process.

REVIEW FIRST

The intent of this book is to make you believe that you *should*, and *can*, have a home that is easy to care for and a pleasure to be in. It's not necessary to accept a plan and design that offers less. Efficiency, function, easy cleaning, low maintenance, atmosphere, excitement, and quiet pleasure — they can all be yours. *But you must be involved in the process.*

Make a List

Review the chapter topics, one by one, from storage and cleaning, to furnishings and outside factors. Make a list. Include each of the items you want to stress in new home planning. Add your own ideas and items to those I have presented.

Priorities

The home renovation book, *Discover Your Dream House*, sets out a check list method for deciding priorities. We discuss each area of the home to pinpoint which changes are needed or what additions to make. With a new home, the method is similar.

Make a list. (It always sounds like too much work to make lists, yet it *saves so much* in the long run.) Use this book for motivation and early direction. List each area desired in your future home, and note the desired function and features of each area. Note how you want each area situated in relation to other areas. Finally, set priorities on all functions and features to establish the must *haves* for your new home.

You may be thinking, about now, that this sounds like too much work. Please be patient in this important stage. It goes quickly and from this information the design concept will grow. If design sketching begins too soon, costly changes will have to be made later, or you will live with mistakes.

Let your mind roam freely in this early thinking stage. It is better to scale down later from exciting ideas than never to have had them.

I don't advocate throwing caution to the wind in your early planning, but simply that you don't constrain your initial thinking. Too often, good planning ideas are rejected before they can be developed because they *seem* too expensive. It's possible that they represent good value. So let your planning-thinking unfold before deciding on priorities. With priorities set, you can scale down selectively from those big ideas.

Set a Budget

It is seldom that cost is no object. You need to set a realistic budget and then stay with it.

The planning method I have talked about will help you do that. When it comes time to compromise, if you must, it's a matter of deleting those items that are low priority and least effective. If you decide to work with an architect, that process will be done together.

Asked what features were desired in the home, a working woman's housebound husband answered, "Another 1500 square feet." That is a common thought. Unfortunately, the size of your home is one of the factors that influences its cost. On the plus side, one result of *good planning* will be to get more use and pleasure from the square footage you build.

WORKING WITH AN ARCHITECT

Selection

This first step is one of the most important and often most difficult. What architect to choose? In whom to put your faith to create your most important environment? Take it one step at a time and it's not that difficult.

Choosing a relative or the friend of a friend is not always the best way. Let's look at another approach.

Compile a list of architects who do residential work. Ask the architects for a list of projects they have done, with owners' names. Call the owners for reference, and look at the homes, if you can. (If the owners are happy with the home, they usually will let you look.)

Invest a little time to find homes that you like. You don't have to love them — they were not designed for you. But look carefully at the basic design. Does the floor plan work well for the owner's use? Does it relate well to its site? And so on. It's important to see enough to make a judgment on quality, owner satisfaction, and your own reaction to the work.

Narrowing down the list, meet with the architects, discuss your thinking, ask questions, and gauge reactions. Check out the chemistry. Through the course of planning, drawings, and construction, you will be working together a long time. It's important that you get along.

The Fee

After you select the architect whose work and personality you like, discuss the fee. Traditional methods of payment for architectural services are: (1) a percentage of the project construction cost; (2) a fixed fee established at the beginning of the project; (3) services provided at hourly rates; (4) a combination of the above, which might happen if extra work is involved beyond your initial agreement.

The three basic phases of the architect's work are: (1) design phase; (2) construction documents phase — working drawings and specifications; (3) construction phase. The architect also can help you obtain bids for construction and select a contractor.

Planning and Design

Once an agreement is secured and the architect begins work, *you must participate.* As stated throughout this book — make your needs and wishes known! Be as informative, helpful, and straightforward as you can. The more input you give the architect during the planning phase, the more effectively the work will progress through each phase thereafter.

Provide all the information you have, including your financial budget. Don't be coy about available funds. An architect, in a position to help you spend wisely, must know how much is to be spent. No one can guarantee what construction will cost, but design work should be based on a realistic target amount.

Remain Open Minded

It's fine to show an architect photographs of houses, parts of houses, materials, windows, details, etc., that you like. It's a way of providing information about your taste, preference, and experience. However, please don't assume any of it should be duplicated in your own home. Such information becomes counter productive to a good designer when it becomes a design *requirement* that it be copied.

In other words, if you are having a romance with a particular architectural style, and insist upon it for your own house, the result may be mediocre, at best. The rash of trendy "post modern" buildings sweeping the country attests to that. Good design doesn't need stimulus from a specific period, like "Greek Revival" or "English Tudor." The house form should be developed from the conditions and requirements of the project as a whole.

Nor is it required that you attempt rough design sketches of your own. The designer can develop ideas based on your needs, desires, and priorities. To that end, it's better not to become attached to an early design attempt of your own. That could prevent you being open minded about a good, but different, design scheme presented by the architect.

Understanding the Design

The day has arrived — you get to see the design drawings! Design drawings, especially floor plans, may be difficult for you to interpret. After all,

it's not the type of thing you look at every day.

Please believe that you have an *obligation* to ask the architect to clarify *anything* you don't understand. This is not the time to be bashful or too proud to admit you don't understand all aspects of the design drawings. It's a disservice to you both to let the architect think you understand and approve, if there is something you don't grasp. The architect can't always read your mind!

Visualizing the Space

To visualize space in three dimensions is difficult for most people. Here is a little exercise that might help you to "walk through" the spaces shown in a floor plan.

As you look at the plan, imagine yourself in different locations within the rooms. For example, you may be sitting in a chair facing a fireplace. (Have furniture drawn in to the scale of the plan.) Visualize the walls or objects on each side of the fireplace. Imagine (still looking at the plan) that you get up and walk to another space — kitchen or bedroom. Think about the path of travel — what you do and see in getting there. Look at the doors, windows, or built-in furniture as you "walk" through the spaces.

Follow similar procedures until you feel familiar with the space. Go on to other areas or rooms in a similar manner.

Communication between you and the architect at this stage should be comprehensive. Time spent here helps to avoid future surprises and changes. The next stage of the work converts the design to construction drawings from which your house is built. Changes made after construction starts usually cost extra time and money.

There is another reason you should thoroughly understand the design drawings, before approval. From these drawings the architect will prepare construction drawings, which are more complex. Design *changes* made during the construction drawing phase can be costly to the architect.

Construction Drawings

Here the architect and consultants prepare detailed drawings and specifications. From there, contractors' bids are taken and actual construction is performed.

During the construction drawings phase you will have periodic, but less, involvement. It's a good time for you to begin setting up your financing for construction. Also, this is a the time to make decisions about furnishings for your house.

Bidding for Construction

Drawings and specifications build your house on paper, but it's still only paper. The next step is to bid the project and select a contractor to actually build it.

Consulting with your architect, select the contractors to bid the construction. Select contractors *of similar high quality.* To include one bidder of marginal quality may erode the serious intent of good bidders. Therefore, they might not spend the time required to give you a competitive bid.

Check them out. Check their financial references and record, for stability. Get a list of completed projects with owners' names for reference. Qualify their capabilities and reputation *before* asking them to bid. You then can feel more assurance about selecting the lowest bidder.

Having selected bidders wisely, usually you accept the lowest bid. Consult with your architect and attorney for assistance in contractor selection and awarding the contract for construction. Also, consult with your insurance advisor for owner's protection during the bidding process.

Note: The final chapters of *Discover Your Dream House* provide more detailed guidelines for bidding, awarding the contract, and the construction process.

CONSTRUCTION

The process of communication continues to be very important. Ask your architect to outline the events forthcoming in the construction phase. Discuss in detail the procedures to follow during construction. Have a clear understanding of the separate responsibilities of each party — you the owner, the architect, and the contractor.

Communication is Key

There is no such thing as a guarantee of success, in your relationship with your architect, or in construction. However, as with all relationships, the basics apply: common sense, fairness, mutual trust, understanding of responsibilities and — always — *constant communication.*

20
Being Content Doesn't Mean You're Perfect

To gain full benefit from this book, you must believe that you *deserve* time for yourself. You must believe a beautiful home can be yours.

To insist on features that promote convenience and easy cleaning in your home, first overcome the feeling that all time should be spent working — being "productive."

YOU DON'T HAVE TO BE PERFECT

At least eighteen million families in America are two-worker families. About fourteen million of those families have children. By the end of the century, women will make up about fifty percent of the labor force in America.

Another important statistic is that most women in these eighteen million "two-worker" families are still doing the housework themselves.

It would seem that a contented "working woman" is the one who arrives at a balance — a balance between the workplace and home, and what happens in each place.

That woman's home probably is clean, but not always "spotless." Also, she might have discovered that she can't be all things to all people at all times. She is not perfect.

LET'S ALL TAKE PART

This same "contented" woman knows that all others in her sphere need to share in the *pleasures* of the home.

"Working Woman's Dream House" should be everyone's special environment, where all members enjoy good design and more "quality time." The need for convenience, interaction, aesthetic pleasure, and private space is universal.

ABOUT THE BOOK

It isn't possible to touch all bases, list every situation, or solve every problem in one book. And, it is eminently a fact, we are all different. Varying degrees of comfort, convenience, and aesthetic pleasure satisfy each of us. So, knowing yourself well, and those around you, take from the book what gives the most benefit to your most important environment — your home.

Glossary

ABUT — Join one end of a material to another material.

ACCENT LIGHTING — Directional lighting to emphasize a particular object.

ACOUSTICAL — Material with sound absorbing qualities.

ANCHOR BOLT — Threaded steel rod inserted in a masonry wall or concrete footing to anchor ledgers or plates.

BACKFILL — Replacing excavated earth, usually against foundation or stem wall, or in a ditch.

BALUSTER — Any of the small posts under a railing in a staircase.

BASEBOARD (Base) — Trim or finish material at intersection of floor and wall.

BATTEN — Strip of wood, usually vertical, covering a joint or used in a series as part of a design.

BEAM — Horizontal member, structurally supporting a load.

BEARING PARTITION — Interior wall which supports a load.

BOARD FOOT — Unit of measurement for wood quantity, 1" thick, 12" wide and 12" long.

BRACE — Stabilizing member used to stiffen a portion of a structure.

BRICK VENEER — Brick facing.

BRIDGING — Cross bracing used between joists.

BTU — British Thermal Unit, a unit for measuring heat.

BUILT-UP-ROOF — Layers of roofing felts and asphaltic compound.

CANT — Angular member used under finish roofing, normally to eliminate right angle at intersection of roof and wall.

CANTILEVER — A beam secured at one end, extending over and projecting from a support.

CASEMENT — A window frame that opens from hinges on the side.

CAULKING — Compound used to seal or waterproof joints or cracks.

CENTER TO CENTER — Also noted as C.C., measurement from center of one member to center of another.

CLERESTORY — (Clearstory) The upper portion of a building (space) with windows above adjacent roofs.

COLUMN — A vertical structural member supporting a load.

CONTROL JOINT — A linear space separating areas of material that helps to control the location of cracking due to expansion and contraction.

COPING — The capping or covering to a wall.

CORBEL — Portion of building material projecting from a wall, sometimes used for support.

COUNTERSINK — Recessing the head of a screw, nail or bolt.

COVE LIGHTING — Lighting shielded by a horizontal ledge or recess, distributing light on upper wall and ceiling.

CRAWL SPACE — Shallow access space, usually between ground and floor framing.

CRICKET — Pitch in roof to divert water.

DIRECT LIGHTING — At lease 90% of emitted light is directed toward the surface to be illuminated.

DORMER — A window in a sloping roof.

DOUBLE HUNG — Describes a window divided horizontally, both top and bottom sections of which operate up and down.

DOWNLIGHT — A small, direct light fixture — recessed, surface mounted, or suspended.

DOWNSPOUT — A pipe, usually metal or plastic, which carries water from gutters or roof drains to the ground.

DRY WALL — (Gypsum board) sheets of paper covered plaster.

DUCT — A tube or conduit which conveys and distributes air for heating or air conditioning. Also refers to a wire conduit.

EASEMENT — A right which one has in the land of another; as a right of way, access to water, power, etc.

EAVES — The lower part of a roof projecting beyond the face of the wall.

ELEVATION — The surface or face of something (building, interior wall, etc.) viewed straight on, without perspective.

FACADE — The elevation or main face of a building.

FASCIA — A vertical band, usually with a small projection, at the edge of a roof.

FLASHING — Metal or other sheet material used in wall or roof construction to keep out moisture.

FOOTING — A thickened section of concrete, wider than the foundation wall or column it supports.

FOUNDATION — The supporting part of a structure, below the floor system and below grade.

FURRING — Wood or metal strips fastened to wall or ceiling over which a finish material will be placed.

GABLE — The sloping ends of a ridged roof and the triangular segment of wall they enclose.

GLAZING — Glass set into window frames or openings.

GROUT — A thinned mortar used to fill voids and cavities in masonry.

GYPSUM BOARD — (Dry wall) Sheets of paper covered plaster.

HARDWARE — Exposed metal parts of a house, such as doorknobs and locks, door and window hinges, levers, cabinet hinges, drawer pulls, etc.

HEAD — Horizontal section at the top of a wall opening (i.e., top section of a door or window).

HIPPED ROOF — Roof sloping on four sides.

HOSE BIBB — End of water pipe, threaded for hose connection, on an outside wall.

INCANDESCENT LAMP — Normal light bulb in every day use.

INDIRECT LIGHTING — The greater percentage of light is emitted upward.

INSULATION — A material with high resistance to transmission of heat or cold.

JALOUSIE — Narrow glass slats in windows, usually operable.

JAMB — Sides of door and window.

JOIST — Member, in a series of members, used to support floor, ceiling, or roof.

KEYSTONE — The central stone of a semicircular arch.

LAG SCREW — Square or hexagonal headed wood screw, normally used for heavy duty.

LAMINATE — Layers of material bonded together.

LANDING — A platform at the end of a flight of stairs or between flights of stairs.

LEDGER — Wood member anchored to wall, used for supporting end of joist.

LIEN WAIVER — In construction, a document attesting that a party has been paid for labor and materials.

LINTEL — Horizontal structural member spanning an opening.

LOAD BEARING WALL — Wall supporting a load.

MANSARD — A four sided roof with two slopes each side, the lower slope being steeper than the upper.

MECHANICAL EQUIPMENT — Heating, ventilating, and air conditioning equipment.

MILLWORK — Finished wood work and products that usually require refinement and attention to detail. Items include door and window frames, trim, moldings, paneling, balusters, and hand rails.

MODULAR — Repeated units of divisible measurement.

MOLDING — A linear trim material, usually with a curved surface, used for decoration or to cover a joint.

MULLION — Vertical member separating two or more windows.

NONBEARING PARTITION — An interior wall supporting its own weight, but no other load.

NONBEARING WALL — A wall supporting its own weight and no other load.

PARAPET — A wall projecting above the roof.

PARTITION — Interior dividing wall.

PENNY — Refers to nail length. For instance, a 10 penny nail is 3 inches long.

PIER — A mass of masonry, as distinct from a column, used for structural support.

PITCH — Slope in a roof.

PLATE — Horizontal member, usually wood, directly under wall studs, joists, or roof trusses.

PLUMB — Vertically level or true.

POINTING — To mortar fill crevices or voids in the joints of a masonry wall.

PROGRAM — A written description of requirements for a building or project. Requirements are based on needs and desires of building occupants.

RAFTER — Normally a roof timber that extends from the ridge to the eaves.

REBAR — Abbreviation for steel reinforcing bar used in concrete or grouted masonry walls to provide tensile strength.

RESILIENT — Ability to return to original shape.

RIDGE — Apex of a sloping roof, running from end to end.

RISER — The vertical portion of a step, between treads.

RUSTICATION — Masonry or stonework with roughened surfaces and recessed joints.

SCALE — The proportion that the building in a drawing bears to the real building it represents (i.e., ¼ inch equals one foot).

SCUTTLE — An opening in ceiling or roof for access.

SET BACK — The required distance for separating building construction from a property line.

SHAKE — Wood shingles, hand split.

SHEATHING — Material covering joists, rafters, or studs, used under the finished material.

SHIM — A wedge or filler.

SOFFIT — Underside of exterior overhang.

SOLE — Flat horizontal member under studs.

SPECIFICATIONS — Written instructions and description of building materials, methods and installation.

STUDS — Vertical members in wall framing.

SUB FLOOR — Material under the finish floor.

TOE NAIL — Nail driven in at an angle.

TONGUE-AND-GROOVE JOINT — A joint in which the tongue of one board fits into the groove of another.

TREAD — The horizontal portion of a stair.

TRUSS — A rigid framework of members for supporting the roof, usually bearing on outside walls.

VAPOR BARRIER — A water resistant membrane.

VENT — A pipe or opening which allows flow of air.

WEATHERSTRIP — Sealing material used at doors and windows.

Index